THE SWITCH ON YOUR BRAIN™ 5 STEP LEARNING PROCESS

LEARN HOW TO LEARN

BY

DR. CAROLINE LEAF

First published by Switch On Your Brain Pty(ltd.) 2007
2nd edition Published by Switch On Your Brain USA 2009

© Dr. Caroline Leaf

For further information on "Switch On Your Brain" training, contact by phone:
917.251.5069

E-mail: caroline@drleaf.net, or visit the website: www.drleaf.net

EDITING: Carolyn Haggard

INTERIOR DESIGN and LAYOUT: Inprov

COVER DESIGN, LAYOUT and EDITING: Inprov

ISBN: 987-0-9800638-6-8

Dedication

To all of you out there who have thought you couldn't learn,

NOW you can . . . it's easy!

To my amazing family who faithfully use "Mom's" system . . .

thank you Jessica, Dominique, Jeffrey-John and Alexandria for your

support. I am so proud of how you have literally "proved"

that the Switch On Your Brain™ 5 Step Learning Process works!

And to Mac, my brilliant, special husband . . . you have been intimately

involved in my research for 20 years; you're my greatest fan . . .

well, I am also yours!

Table of Contents

Chapter 1

THE TRUTH ABOUT YOUR AMAZING BRAIN

The 5 steps of the Switch On Your Brain™ 5 Step Learning System are based scientifically on how the brain functions. That's why these 5 steps to exam success are "brain friendly" – they work with, and not against, the natural functioning of the brain.

Traditional study methods like reading and rereading, taking summary notes and learning them by heart, rote learning, and using memory tricks are not "brain compatible." These techniques work against the natural functioning of the brain, and that is why studying can be so difficult!

If you want to remember something and apply that knowledge in an exam and retain that information for long periods of time, then working with how your brain functions naturally will make the learning process much less stressful.

One of the most incredible things about the brain is that it has been proved scientifically that thinking and learning can turn our genes on or off, shaping our brain anatomy and behavior. This idea that the brain can change its own structure and function through thought and activity is vitally important to successful learning, because it means that you can grow your own brain at will. So wherever you are as a learner, you can improve your brain function, and if you take advantage of the way your brain builds memory, you can't help but succeed!

HOW DOES THE BRAIN WORK?

In order to answer the question of what the brain's natural functioning looks like, let's have a quick biology lesson.

I am sure that you are aware of the common perception that the left side of the brain controls more academic type functions and the right side controls the more creative functions.

However, this is really a misconception because brain research over the years demonstrates that the right brain vs. the left brain theory is unscientific!

According to the latest research on the brain (including over the past 20 years my own research of many renowned brain researchers), we have missed it when it comes to understanding the brain.

The truth is that both sides of the brain do everything. This means that when you are doing math, science or history, both the left and right sides are working. The same applies to all the other subjects. I can use a simple analogy to demonstrate this point.

CONSIDER: 2 X 2=4

I am sure you will agree that 2 x 2 = 4 and that 4 = 2 groups of 2. This simple times table demonstrates how the brain processes information.

How? Quite simply: the left side of the brain processes information from the detail (2 x 2) to the big picture (= 4); the right side of the brain processes the same information, but from the big picture (4) to the detail (= 2 groups of 2). When you put these two together, you have deep understanding. If you don't, you will only have partial understanding.

THE PUZZLE

Another way of understanding how the left and right sides of the brain function is by doing a jigsaw puzzle. As you complete the puzzle, you probably keep in view the picture of the puzzle as a reference, and you most likely sort the pieces based on similarity of color and picture etc.

Next, you most likely start by selecting a single piece – the detail – then looking at where it fits into the big picture of the puzzle, and continue to build the puzzle piece by piece. In this process, you are continually moving between the detail of the single puzzle piece to the big picture of the puzzle and back to the detail again as you continue to build.

DETAIL TO BIG PICTURE AND BIG PICTURE TO DETAIL

The left-brain processes from the detail to the big picture, and the right brain processes from big picture to the detail. You need to use both sides of the brain when building the puzzle. You cannot build it properly using only the left or right side.

This same process applies to learning and is the basis for the Switch On Your Brain™ 5 Step Leaning Process. The strengths of each side of our brain need to work in synergy, at the same time, in order to best harness the power of our brain. Moving from detail to the big picture (left side of the brain) needs to be integrated back from the big picture to the detail (right side of the brain) at the same time.

Remember: 2 x 2 = 4 is the same as 4 = 2 groups of 2. Rote learning and other traditional study methods do not compare the detail to the big picture and the big picture to the detail at the same time. This is why these traditional study methods do not really work and why most learners "cram" just before exams.

Incorrect studying is hard because a student is most often trying to cram in lots of detail without really understanding the information. This is only one side of the story or one perspective – details that may not be linked in our brains to the big picture. Because of the brain's incredible capacity, sometimes we can get by on an exam when studying incorrectly, but this is certainly not the best option. We won't retain the important information for very long; plus, it can be extremely stressful! Easy-come easy-go is the law of the brain!

THE CORPUS CALLOSUM – THE LIGHT SWITCH OF THE BRAIN

The key to linking the two sides of our brain to work together is the corpus callosum. Although it sounds intimidating, it actually is quite amazing! This structure in the middle of the brain integrates the two different perspectives – the detail to the big picture and the big picture to the detail – together. We'll learn more about this in the next chapter. Now, it's important to know that the corpus callosum acts like a light switch, literally switching on the brain and allowing the two sides to work together.

The corpus callosum is a very important part of the brain because it intellectualizes and thinks about the two perspectives of information. It is also involved, along with other brain structures, in selecting what information to store in the brain and comparing new information to what is already in the brain.

Every bit of information we are exposed to goes into our brain in duplicate – one memory on each side of the brain. This means we have two connected memories of everything – each memory supplying a different perspective. When these two perspectives are put together by the corpus callosum, we get an "AH-HA experience," meaning we have understood! The light is "switched on." The opposite is also true, if the two perspectives of the same memory are not put together properly, then our level of understanding drops.

The answer to sustainable learning, is to get the two sides of the brain working together through the corpus callosum – the light switch – so we can get a good understanding of the concepts we are learning. Brain research has also shown that the only way to build a good, lasting memory of material we have read is through good understanding.

Quite simply, good understanding means good memory; poor understanding means bad memory. Good understanding happens when both sides of the brain are working together properly; poor understanding happens when both sides of the brain are not working together properly. To get the two sides of the brain working together requires deep intellectual ongoing thought.

THE INCREDIBLE CAPACITY OF THE BRAIN

Did you know that the average person only uses around 0.001 percent of the brain for intellectual functioning? We are grossly under-using our brains. We are born with approximately 200 billion nerve cells in our brains. We lose 100 billion through a refining process by the time we are two years of age. After that, we do not lose more unless we experience a traumatic accident or take drugs or alcohol.

As we learn new bits of information, the nerve cells (which, by the way, look like trees) grow branches, a new branch for every new piece of information. These branches are actually your memories; we call them the "magic trees of the mind." The more branches on the tree, and the more connections they make to other branches, the more memory we build and more intelligent we become. This process continues throughout our lives, so we grow branches till we die!

One nerve cell in the brain is able to grow approximately 15,000 to 200,000 branches. This is about the amount of facts contained in one twelfth grade subject! This means that it would take an average of three million years to fill up one human brain!

You will never run out of storage space in the brain. It has an infinite capacity to learn and store. When we learn, we are growing branches on the nerve cells, as opposed to new nerve cells, and the capacity to grow branches is infinite! Research shows thinking and learning can turn our genes on or off, shaping our behavior, so the brain can change its own structure and function (for better or worse) through thought and activity! This is where free will steps in.

MAGIC TREES OF THE MIND

So when you feel like you cannot fit another thing into your brain, it's not because it's full; it's because you have built your memory poorly.

Since memory building is so crucial, we will explore exactly how to build good memory in chapter 2.

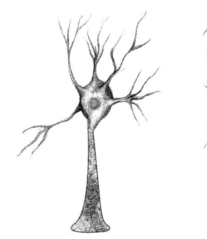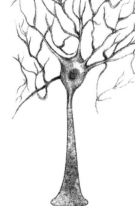

Notes and Summary:

Notes and Summary:

Chapter 2

WHAT IS MEMORY, AND HOW DO WE MAKE IT WORK?

Let's begin this discussion on memory by first exploring the corpus callosum and the surrounding areas a little more. This C-shaped structure is in the middle of the brain and connects both the left and the right sides of the brain. We touched upon the corpus callosum briefly in Chapter 1, but since this is such an exciting part of our brain function, it is important to become familiar with it.

The "Thinking Areas" of the Brain

The corpus callosum is the complex network of fibers connecting the two sides of the brain. It, and the network of surrounding connections, forms a hub that integrates information, enabling the two sides of the brain to work together. It is here that sustainable learning truly starts to happen.

The two sides of the brain work by using mirror-imaging. For every bit of information on the left side, there is the exact same information on the right side, but in mirror image format – left is detail to big picture, and right is big picture to detail. We build memory "in stereo." It is the corpus callosum and the surrounding areas that get these stereo memories working together. It directly influences how well memory is built.

We are using both sides of the brain most of the time as we build new memory and use existing memory – they cannot be turned off. The brain literally practices thinking when you are not aware of it, even while you are sleeping. The corpus callosum allows the two sides of the brain to "talk" to each other, integrating and comparing information. We could call the corpus callosum and its interaction with the surrounding areas (thalamus, hypothalamus, hippocampus, entorrhinal cortex, amygdala) our "thinking areas."

The more efficiently the corpus callosum operates (this is up to you as there is infinite potential), the more efficient our understanding and thinking and learning becomes, the better the memory we build. Using mainly the left side of the brain for learning, with only limited involvement of the right side, limits the quality and type of information processed, leading to rote type learning and inferior stereotyped thinking. This is what happens when we use the wrong study methods!

 How do this incredible structure and the equally incredible surrounding areas actually "think and integrate" information across the two sides of the brain and assist in building memory and switching the brain on? Let's move to the next section to see how this all comes together.

HOW DO WE BUILD MEMORY?

In the process of understanding, using the corpus callosum with the rest of the brain, our mind goes through very distinctive processes. We receive "data" and information 24 hours a day from all of our senses. All of the information we acquire from birth to death goes into our brain and is stored on the little branches growing out of the nerve cells in the brain.

NERVE CELL

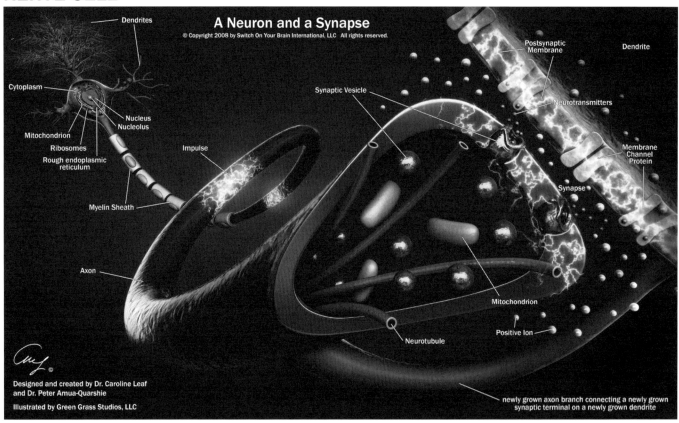

A Neuron and a Synapse
© Copyright 2008 by Switch On Your Brain International, LLC All rights reserved.

Designed and created by Dr. Caroline Leaf and Dr. Peter Amua-Quarshie
Illustrated by Green Grass Studios, LLC

The information that grows onto these nerve cells in our brain looks a lot like trees in a forest. We call these "memory-trees" the "magic trees of the mind" because they can store an unlimited amount of information! Problems with memory and thinking do not come from a lack of storage space in the brain, but rather from the way in which information is put into the brain – that is, how we actually build memory.

It is, therefore, a matter of building memory or inputting information into the brain correctly so it can be accessed easily. This literally means growing branches on the neuron trees. Look on the previous page at the picture of a nerve cell – it has lots of branches and is a good memory. Branches can get lost and connections interlinking information in the brain can melt away due to poor methods of learning and studying. Look at the picture of the 2 nerve cells below: the first is a good memory; the second with less branches is a weaker memory where information has been lost. Good memory means growing multiple branches that don't fall off your trees and having lots of connections between the trees! That is exactly what the Switch On Your Brain™ 5 Step Learning Process (chapter 5) is going to teach you to do. So read on . . .

DENDRITES

Information is useless unless it is processed correctly and understandably. Information understood to the point that it can be used or applied results in the intelligent use of knowledge. Building memory is predominantly about understanding. As you think hard about information with the objective of understanding, major consolidation of memory branches and connections occurs and information is converted from short-term memory to long-term memory. You will hold onto what you have learned and be able to use it only with sustained practice and deep understanding.

Branches grow on the nerve cell in response to information coming into the brain, but how well they grow and efficiently connect to other neurons containing related information depends on how well you think – the more efficiently you think, the more you will understand, the more the genes will turn on the protein synthesis. All this fancy scientific talk means you grow a stable branch that is consolidated and the memory becomes one you can use!

The branches store this information in electrical format, one concept per branch. The information we process is from the 5 senses. All of this is changed in the eye and ear and the other sense receptors in the body into electrical impulses and, like all electrical impulses, has to flow along some sort of conductor.

In the case of the brain, the conductor happens to be neurons with little branches called dendrites and longer branches called axons (look at the image on page 19). Dendrites and axons grow in response to incoming data that is converted to electrical impulses.

Intelligence can actually be seen in the brain! The more densely organized the dendritic arrangement – the thickly branched "magic tree" – the more connected and intelligent the memory. Great memories look like big bushy trees. Weaker memories look like straggly small thin trees.

The brain really is incredible; if you remember from chapter one, it grows a double connected memory of everything – one magic tree in the left side of the brain and another magic tree of the same information in the right. We build all memories in duplicate – the one side provides the detail to the big picture and the other side the big picture to the detail, just like a mirror image.

SHORT AND LONG-TERM MEMORY

Although we may not think of it often, memory figures centrally in all our abilities. It lies at the heart of our ability to understand written and spoken language because it enables us to identify words, to ascribe meaning to visual or auditory patterns, and to integrate the meanings of individual words into connected speech. Similarly, it is critical in movement control and writing, in recognizing a friend's face, forming mental images and so much more.

For example, right now, as you read this chapter, you are growing dendrites (discussed above) to accommodate the information you are selecting, thus growing a memory. This initial "building-phase" is known as short-term memory and happens more or less as follows: the information pours from the entorrhinal cortex into the hippocampus, a tube-like structure surrounding the corpus-callosum; then these three structures along with the frontal lobe and amygdala and a few other parts of the brain (see the image in the beginning of chapter 8) "read" and "intellectualize" the information.

How well this is done depends on our free will. Geneticists working on the gene code have found that there are genes that create what we know as free will. This gene code is thought to be located in the DNA of nerve cells in the corpus callosum and in the front of the brain, because this area is where decision making and executive type functions take place. This is supported by the research on the neuroplasticity of the brain that tells us the brain physically changes according to how we think! Thus the corpus callosum works with the front of the brain, known as the frontal lobe, in refining memory building. The more we choose to think and intellectualize, the better the memory we build – you can choose to think or not to think!

If you choose to think deeply (using the corpus callosum) and understanding takes place, the little branches (dendrites) that grow will be firmly attached. If, however, there was not good understanding of the information, the little branches grown will be unstable and hang loosely. These unstable branches affect the emotions.

After 24-48 hours, while you are sleeping, little "vacuum-cleaners" (glial cells in the brain) remove the unstable branches and place them into inaccessible memory – the "recycle bin." The glial cells "sort out your thinking" as you sleep. The information here becomes recognizable in the sense that you would have heard or seen the information before, but it will not be usable. This is forgetting.

Whatever dendrites are left on the nerve cell will then form long-term memory. In the image on page 21 some memories are more branched than others – the bushier memories are the stronger memories. Research has shown that if memory is not built correctly (i.e. the corpus callosum and surrounding areas integrating the two side of the brain and processing the information until it is understood) then between 35 percent to 75 percent of the memory may be forgotten within 24 to 48 hours!

Therefore short-term memory is when we build memory that lasts for 24 to 48 hours. Long-term memory is not another physical location in the brain but what is left on the "memory tree" after 48 hours.

FORGETTING

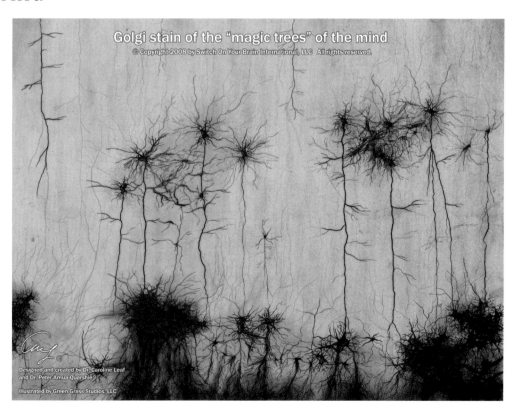

Up to 35 percent to 75 percent of information can be lost if the memory is incorrectly built.

Summary

We have short-term memory (where our memories are built) and long-term memory (what is left of the memories after 24-48 hours and stored permanently). In order to build a good memory that can be used in both short and long-term memory, we have to understand the information with which we are trying to build the memory.

 If you understand the material, then you will automatically build a good stable memory. If, on the other hand, you do not understand the material, you will still build a memory, but it will be unstable and could easily fall apart.

Memories live in a short-term state for about 24 to 48 hours, after which the brain's natural "vacuum cleaners" (glial cells) come along to clean up all unstable memories (information not really understood). Glial cells literally "sort out" your thinking. The "cleaned up" unstable memories are then emptied into the "trash can" of the brain – they are not thrown out your ears! The reason for this is that unstable memories will disturb the natural biochemical functioning of the brain and are thus "cleaned up." When something is in the "trash can" of the brain, we are able to recognize the information but unable to use it.

The Switch On Your Brain™ 5 Step Learning Process will ensure that you build good, useful and intelligent memory using your corpus callosum properly!

Let's dive into these 5 steps . . .

Notes and Summary:

Notes and Summary:

Chapter 3

ATTITUDE

Attitude is everything! In fact, your attitude is so powerful that it can strongly impact the success of your learning.

Attitude is very closely linked to motivation and free will. Your attitude can also be considered your "state of mind." Let's look at where attitude lives in the brain, because it is always much easier to understand something when you can see it or at least try to visualize it.

Information goes into your brain as electrical impulses gathered through your five senses – sight, sound, taste, touch, smell – they all gather at an area that is like a doorway in your brain. This doorway and its surrounding areas have a strange name, the entorrhinal cortex.

The information then shoots through to the middle of your brain, which is like a big chemical factory. This is where chemicals are squirted out to start digesting the information from your five senses coming in through the doorway.

In order to do this, the information is first shot to the top part of the brain where all your memories are stored – we call this area the cortex of the brain, and since it looks like a big forest, it is referred to as the "magic trees" of the mind.

These aren't actually trees; they are memories. We call these memories "trees" because that's exactly they look like, huge bushy trees (we reviewed these previously in chapters 1 and 2).

The information flies through these magic trees – your memories – alerting them to the new incoming information, very much like a preview of a movie. This is the first place where attitude is activated; it is literally "switched on" as the information sweeps through the magic trees like a breeze ("the breeze through the trees").

It may land on a similar memory. If it's a good memory, you will experience a subtle warm and happy feeling just outside of your conscious mind. If the memory is negative, feelings of turbulence will start and you will find your peace disturbed. This is the first point where your attitude begins to develop on a non-conscious level. You can't quite identify it yet, but something is starting to happen.

STEP ONE

The first step in controlling attitude is to respond to this quickening. Start to analyze this quickening, this witness in you, and bring it into your conscious awareness. The excitement in you is responding to knowledge. Our brains are designed to respond to knowledge, and you need to detect whether this information is positive or negative for you. The purpose of identifying this quickening is to protect and guard your mind because, quite simply, trash in, trash out.

What does this mean? It means that if the incoming knowledge and thoughts are good, like your learning material, your intellect will be developed, but if the information is negative and fear-based, chemicals that disrupt thinking are released into the brain.

The "preview" of the information will influence how you start to feel about the information. It's quite subtle, not quite a conscious thought yet, but the factory of the brain is very aware of these emotions and is programmed to respond to the information coming in from the magic trees. How does it do this? The factory literally squirts out chemicals that correspond to your non-conscious emotions and feelings about the incoming information. So if you feel happy, a certain group of chemicals is secreted; if you feel angry, another group of chemicals is squirted, and so on.

When these chemicals start flowing, an attitude – either positive or negative – is about to develop, because these little chemicals, called "molecules of emotion," carry the emotions you are feeling inside them. They carry these emotions all the way into another part of your brain, just below the chemical factory. This is the library of the brain. It has a very formal sounding name, amygdala, but is only about the size of an almond.

Then, once the package of information and chemicals hits this library, you really feel something. You will feel a strong very conscious emotion in reaction to the thoughts that were activated in the magic trees of the mind and the molecules of emotion.

It may sound contrary to what you've been taught, but the key is not to react. That's because even though it may feel like your emotions are based on truth, this library functions based upon perceptions. For every memory that you build, you will have a feeling attached to it that is stored in your library. The key to remember is that this feeling is not always based upon the truth, and a lot of the time, the emotions in this library are quite dangerous if you follow them or allow them to control you.

For example, you may be scared of math; as soon as you walk into the math class, anxiety and fear well up in you, resulting in a negative attitude. This negative attitude will block your ability to take in the information during the lesson. So it is really important that you deal with the emotion activated, or it will control you!

STEP TWO

Step two in dealing with attitude is to acknowledge and analyze the strong emotion you are feeling. Don't react to it, think first and if possible, put it "back on the shelf" and tell yourself something positive like, "I don't like math because I think I'm not so good at it, but I am going to conquer this fear, face it and ask questions till I do understand."

You need to acknowledge how you feel, then put the feeling back on the shelf. Emotions cannot be buried because they are alive.

If you let the emotions control you, your brain will secrete anger and fear chemicals that will put your body into a stress reaction (see chapter 8). Once your body is in a stress reaction, you develop a negative or bad attitude from all these chemicals flowing, making you think negatively, which starts the whole reaction again. This will go on and on until you stop the cycle.

If you don't control these first reactive emotions, you will start feeling depressed which makes your attitude even more negative. Never let your emotions control you. Your intellectual processes will be affected, making learning difficult.

Now let's move to the next step.

Information passes from the library into a garden-hose like structure called the hippocampus. The information flows through the hippocampus, much like water flowing through a garden hose. This garden hose surrounds the corpus callosum (mentioned earlier) that holds the two sides of the brain together – one of the corpus callosum's many functions. The corpus callosum is activated or awakened as the information flows through the garden hose (hippocampus), but only as much as you allow it to be activated. This is because the corpus callosum contains part of the genetic structure for your "free will." Genes are quite literally turned on and off as you think.

We are all individuals and like to make our own choices. No one can force you to do anything; no one can override your free will. This free will is in your corpus callosum and the front part of your brain. In terms of learning, free will plays a big role, because if you choose not to listen to what your teacher or lecturer is explaining, major things happen in your brain that put your body into a stress reaction, which in turn, blocks memory building. The choices you make will influence how well you block a memory of something.

Let's have a look at what happens in your brain when the garden hose (hippocampus) fills up with all the information and activates your free will. Whatever choice you make about the information in the garden hose using your free will is going to be directly linked to your attitude. If you choose to let your thoughts run wild and tell yourself things like, "This is so boring. I can't stand this teacher," and so on, you will block the brain's ability to analyze and think about the important information in the garden hose, and only a little bit of it will filter through into the magic trees of the mind where all your memories are. The rest of the information will pour back out of the garden hose and become heat energy!

You can lose up to 35 percent to 75 percent of the information you need just by having a bad attitude as you walk into the classroom. What a waste of time and energy. You will only build good memory if you control the choices you make about those negative thoughts; you can either submit to them or rise above them!

Submitting to them causes chemical chaos in the brain that makes your mind foggy. You lose concentration and will find it difficult to listen to everything the teacher is saying. Quite simply, learning becomes really difficult.

STEP THREE

This step is controlling your thought life.

Therefore step three in controlling your attitude deals with controlling your thought life. You are what you think, and you will become what you think. The more you think about something the more it controls you. Why? Because as you think, you are building memory and reinforcing existing memory and linking networks in your mind – literally growing branches between the trees – and remember, your brain has an unlimited capacity for growing these connections.

Clearly then, what you think determines how you function intellectually, emotionally and physically.

Here are some typical emotionally charged negative thoughts that block good attitude and need to be controlled:

» I just know it won't work.

» I hate school.

» I am not artistic.

- » I just don't have the energy to make a change.

- » I should care about it now, but it'll wait until tomorrow.

- » Nothing ever seems to go right for me.

- » I will start my studies tomorrow.

- » I am just no good at anything.

- » If it weren't for bad luck, I wouldn't have any luck at all.

- » I am at the end of my rope.

- » If only I were smarter.

- » Mondays are never good days for me.

Let's have a look at some positive statements that we could say here to help deal with that first dangerous reactive emotion:

- » I know it will work, because I put all of my effort into making this a success.

- » I am creative in my own way.

- » I have been storing my energy and am ready to handle change.

- » Tomorrow is not guaranteed. I won't put off until tomorrow what I can do today.

- » Today I will be judged by my effort and my positive attitude, which will ensure that every day is a great day.

- » I feel better about myself today, because I know the importance of learning correctly.

- » I'd make a lousy anybody else, but I can be the best me in the world.

- » I don't live my life on luck. I live my life by faith, persistence and a positive attitude.

- » I am enhancing my skills daily and creating opportunities for the future.

- » I can't go to Friday until I step into Monday, and every day is an opportunity.

Let's quickly recap the three steps that we need to use to control our attitude:

1.   Analyze that quickening that you feel – is it good or is it bad?

2.   Don't react to your first emotion – stand back and analyze it first.

3.   Control your thoughts – accept the good uplifting thoughts and reject the negative ones.

Here are some quotes to encourage you to develop a good attitude:

"You are what you think you are, all day long."
— *Ralph Waldo Emerson*

"If you can imagine it, you can achieve it.
If you dream it, you can become it."
— *Keith D. Harrell*

"You are today where your thoughts have brought you.
You will be tomorrow where your thoughts take you."
— *James Allen*

Notes and Summary:

Notes and Summary:

Chapter 4

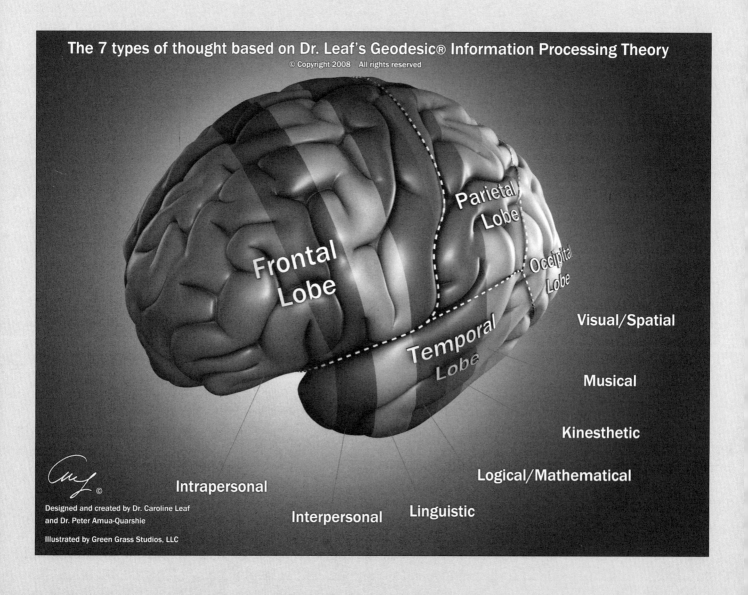

The 7 types of thought based on Dr. Leaf's Geodesic® Information Processing Theory

Frontal Lobe

Parietal Lobe

Occipital Lobe

Temporal Lobe

Visual/Spatial

Musical

Kinesthetic

Logical/Mathematical

Intrapersonal

Interpersonal

Linguistic

Designed and created by Dr. Caroline Leaf
and Dr. Peter Amua-Quarshie

Illustrated by Green Grass Studios, LLC

YOU HAVE 7 TYPES OF THINKING TO HELP YOU SUCCEED IN LEARNING AND IN LIFE

The last (but not least) concept we have to explore in relation to the brain and learning before we jump into the Switch On Your Brain™ 5 Step Learning Process is the concept of the unique gifting.

There are seven different types of thinking, and each one of us has a unique combination of these different types. This unique combination is called our gifting. No two people on the planet have the same thinking combination, which is quite incredible, as it means each and every one of us thinks differently. These differences will affect the way in which we learn and deal with life, because we each have a unique conscious perception of the world.

The subject of thinking and intelligence has been approached in many ways, most of which have led to people being labeled since our natural tendency is to categorize even ideas that cannot be categorized. For example, tests can be taken to label us kinesthetic or linguistic or auditory learners. IQ tests tell us we are gifted or not gifted, verbal or non-verbal. Personality tests telling us we are type A personality or melancholic. Even the multiple intelligence theory is being misunderstood, because people revert back to using one-word descriptions to label people.

All these approaches use one word to describe the unique multifaceted human personality (which with free will is an impossible task). As a result, this is in complete conflict to brain research, which tells us that no two brains are the same, that the brain is neuroplastic and can change with every thought and experience, and that consciousness and the uniqueness of the human mind is named the "hard question" of neuroscience. Brain research does not allow one-label descriptions!

Each of us has to have a little of each of the 7 types of thinking in order to be a rational human being. These are mixed in a uniquely wonderful "cocktail mix" manner – different for each human.

Our "cocktail mix" determines how we cycle through our thoughts to come to an understanding of information and consolidate that memory. The ranking from highest to lowest shows us the order of this cycle, and the order of this cycle is how best you think. Understanding your order helps you understand how you think, which helps you build better memory.

How it works in brain language is the following: as mentioned in chapter one, your brain is made up of approximately 100 billion neurons with the potential to connect approximately 100 trillion times. These 100 billion neurons are clustered into modules or groups that stretch from left to right across the brain. They are not fixed and flow into each other, helping each other especially when the brain has been damaged. Each group has a priority type function. For example, the neurons in the front of the brain – the frontal cortex – deal with decision making, planning, deep analysis, shifting between thoughts, forming goals and sticking to them, developing strategies, and so on; this is called the intrapersonal module. Just behind this area is the interpersonal area responsible for social interaction, communication, turn-taking, tuning into the needs of others. This is followed by the linguistic area which deals with spoken and written language. Then comes the logical/ mathematical area dealing with reasoning, logic, scientific type thought, number, and problem solving. Next is the kinesthetic area that provides awareness of where our limbs are in space, enabling us to control and coordinate movement. Then comes musical, which is musical but also the ability to read between the lines. Finally there is visual/spatial at the back of the brain, which is necessary for forming mental maps in the brain.

How does this thinking cycle work? As you process information, existing memory is activated across all the memory networks in a rolling cyclic way, moving through your ranking from the highest to the lowest. What is the result? You use all 7 types of thought in your "hardwired" order like a well-worn pathway that is a shortcut home. As you think in this natural way, your brain kicks into high gear and you operate like a fine-tuned car with all 7 types of thought oiled into thinking "it" through. When this happens all kinds of great chemicals are squirted through your brain and a frenzy of memory building begins!

My theory, the Geodesic Information Processing theory – in contrast to the IQ and others – looks at the neurological process of thinking and takes into consideration the fact that the brain can change along with our thought life and experience; this is called neuroplasticity.

Instead of taking just a facet and describing the person according to that particular facet, that one single trait, such as linguistic or auditory, my theory of the gifting describes the person in terms of his combination of the 7 different types of thought. These 7 different types of thought are based on the main root functions of the brain and our own unique cycle, creating a unique perception of the world. It is an all encompassing approach.

My theory of the unique gifting of man is based on the functioning of the different parts of the brain and how they all work together to create consciousness. More specifically, my research focuses on the thinking cycle as we process information, because this most accurately portrays the process of getting understanding and building a good memory.

Trying to develop a complex concept and apply it in a practical way can sometimes be a challenge. However, I have created a simple exercise with 70 questions (my abridged profile) that have yes or no answers. After you answer all of the questions, you'll discover the order of your thinking cycle – from the highest to the lowest. But it is important to understand, everyone has all of the seven types of thought in our processing. We all have our own unique order and all types of thinking are touched upon as we process information. These rankings actually give the order that you move through in your thinking cycle.

THE RANKING OF YOUR SCORES INDICATES:

1. Your highest score is the type of thought that you will draw on first – literally the doorway allowing information into your personality.

2. The second highest score is the thinking you draw on to start processing the memory.

3. The third score draws on the type of thinking that will start to consolidate the memory.

4. The fourth confirms the accuracy of memory.

5. The fifth integrates memory building with the other networks in the brain.

6. The sixth leads to the use or application of the memory.

7. Finally, the seventh closes off the cycle of thought as understanding formulates

Your highest score does not simply describe the entirety of who you are; rather, this ranking demonstrates to you how your seven types of thinking work together to describe who you are.

Your gift and the development of your intelligence grow as you allow the seven types of thought to work together. You pass through about 2500 cycles of thought in an hour, which is between 30,000 and 60,000 in a day. This thinking cycle working together activates your gift – the unique you and the particular talents and skills that you have helping your learning. The Switch On Your Brain™ 5 Step Learning Process, in turn, allows your 7 types of thought to work together and actually develop your intelligence.

It is beyond the scope of this workbook to fully analyze your complete gifting profile, so below is a brief description, emphasizing that you need to see yourself as a uniquely gifted individual.

Understanding how you think according to your 7-types-of-thinking gifting profile will help to improve how you use your brain as well as how to learn better. You are unique and gifted. That is the bottom line of what you have been reading up till now. You have a unique pattern of thinking, and in this chapter you can start getting an understanding of all these seven different types of thinking, which will take you toward finding your gift. This is your uniqueness, and it's important to find it and develop it. The 5 steps of the Switch On Your Brain™ Learning Process help you to do so.

You also need to know the order – your pattern of thought – which delineates how your specific gift works. Intelligence is not a static entity, despite what you may have been told in the past. Intelligence is the result of using your seven types of thinking to build great memory that is densely branched and interconnected and therefore extremely useful! Of course, there is a genetic component to your intelligence, but this is just the hard wiring – you are still responsible for finding that gift and unleashing that potential within you. Everyone is gifted, but not everyone uses his or her gift. Always remember: there is something you can do that no one else on this planet can do – it's your responsibility to find this gift and release it. Filling in the profile and applying the Switch On Your Brain™ 5 Step Learning Process to everything will help you do this.

Your thought pattern is not just of one or two types. You could be forgiven for thinking it is, when you look at the overemphasis on logical/mathematical and linguistic types of thinking – this is one of the major weaknesses of traditional schooling systems.

Below is a mini "gift profile" that you can fill in to find your unique gift and find out how you think and learn better.

THE MINI GIFT PROFILE

A few tips to remember:

> This profile is the shortened version and is therefore just an indication or a sampling of your intelligence combination – it is not comprehensive. For the most accurate results, a much more comprehensive evaluation is needed (see my other books).

> There is no wrong answer.

> The quicker you answer the profile and with as little deliberation as possible, the more accurate the answer. If you find yourself debating whether this is like you or not, then it's most likely not and you will check the "no" answer.

> You are not trying to impress anyone – pure honesty is what is required.

> You are not supposed to score high on everything; you are simply looking for your order by scoring.

»   The highest score is the entry point of information

»   The scores will range from high to low showing where your thinking cycle starts and ends and its order. These questions are just a sampling to give you an idea of where your strengths lie. The full profile has about 220 questions. Because there are differences even within the similarities, two people can have similar strengths, but by asking more specific questions, the differences within the similarities will become obvious.

»   When answering the questions the first time, you check yes if the question appeals to you or if it comes naturally. Check no if this is definitely not what you like.

»   When finished, simply add up your checks per section (there are 7 sections – one for each type of thinking) and convert to a percentage (e.g. 7/10 = 70 percent).

»   Then line the scores up from highest to lowest to find your way of thinking – your gift. Your top two types of thinking lead the thinking and memory building process; the other five complete your unique cycle of thought.

1. LINGUISTIC THINKING

1.   I like using stories in order to explain something   ○yes   ○no

2.   I like debating in discussions   ○yes   ○no

3.   I enjoy writing poems, stories, legends, and articles   ○yes   ○no

4.   I would like to write a play   ○yes   ○no

5.   I like telling stories   ○yes   ○no

6.   I like describing events in detail   ○yes   ○no

7.   I like leading discussions   ○yes   ○no

8.   I enjoy writing newsletters   ○yes   ○no

9.   I hear words in my head before I speak, read or write   ○yes   ○no

10. I hear words in my head as I listen to someone or when I am watching TV   ○yes   ○no

SCORE: _____ ÷ 10 X 100 = _____%

2. LOGICAL/MATHEMATICAL THINKING

1.   Mathematical formula "talk" to me – I see meaning in numbers   ○yes   ○no

2. I like creating strategy games like Survivor and treasure hunts ○yes ○no

3. I like hypothesizing – "what if…" ○yes ○no

4. I can always see the pros and cons of a situation ○yes ○no

5. I like planning ○yes ○no

6. I like reasoning things out ○yes ○no

7. I like playing with numbers and doing complex Mathematical operations ○yes ○no

8. I can easily compute numbers in my head ○yes ○no

9. My favorite subjects are or were science, math, and computers ○yes ○no

10. I enjoy solving problems ○yes ○no

SCORE: _____ ÷ 10 X 100 = _____ %

3. VISUAL/SPATIAL THINKING

1. I think in 3-D, for example, I can easily mentally move or manipulate objects in space to see how they will interact with other objects, such as gears turning parts of machinery ○yes ○no

2. I like to produce, and can easily understand graphic information (i.e., using graphs or charts to explain concepts) ○yes ○no

3. I can easily navigate my way through space, for example, when I am moving through openings, moving a car through traffic, or parking a car ○yes ○no

4. I can easily read a road map ○yes ○no

5. I like building Lego, making origami objects, mock houses and bridges ○yes ○no

6. I like building puzzles, especially big ones ○yes ○no

7. I like creating photo collages ○yes ○no

8. I like designing posters/murals/bulletin boards ○yes ○no

9. I find myself visualizing (picturing and imaging) a lot especially when I am listening and trying to understand ○yes ○no

10. I can easily remember large chunks of information (for short periods of time) just from reading ○yes ○no

SCORE: _____ ÷ 10 X 100 = _____ %

4. MUSICAL THINKING

1   I can easily read body language   ⭘yes   ⭘no

2   I find it easy to pick up the nuances in someone's speech, for example whether they are sarcastic, angry, irritated or worried ⭘yes   ⭘no

3.   I find myself listening and responding to a variety of sounds including the human voice, environmental sounds, sounds in nature and music   ⭘yes   ⭘no

4.   I enjoy music and find myself needing it in the learning environment ⭘yes   ⭘no

5.   I will often create my own rhythm if I can't hear music especially when I am concentrating by doing things like clicking my pen, tapping my foot, or rocking in my chair rhythmically   ⭘yes ⭘no

6.   I find myself responding to music by humming along ⭘yes   ⭘no

7.   I find myself responding to music by moving in time to the music   ⭘yes   ⭘no

8.   I find music and singing makes me feel various emotions   ⭘yes   ⭘no

9.   If I watch gymnastics or ballet or dancing or any sport, I can "hear" the music in their body movements   ⭘yes   ⭘no

10. I recognize different types of musical styles and genres and cultural variations   ⭘yes   ⭘no

SCORE: _____ ÷ 10 X 100 = _____ %

5. KINESTHETIC THINKING

1.   I need to explore a new environment through touch and movement   ⭘yes   ⭘no

2.   I like to touch or handle what I need to learn; I cannot just look at it   ⭘yes   ⭘no

3.   I consider myself to be well co-coordinated   ⭘yes   ⭘no

4.   I have a good sense of timing in life. For example, I am always on time and can manage my time ⭘yes   ⭘no

5.   I am good at sports ⭘yes   ⭘no

6.   I am good at arranging furniture in a room, and the placement of ornaments on a table   ⭘yes ⭘no

7.   I enjoy field trips like visiting a museum or the planetarium, and going on camps   ⭘yes   ⭘no

8. I enjoy physical strategy games like "tag," "stuck in the mud," and treasure hunts ◯yes ◯no

9. I notice when people have not color coordinated their clothes, fabrics or styles correctly ◯yes ◯no

10. I find it easy to participate in a group activity that involves a coordinated sequence of movements such as aerobics and dancing ◯yes ◯no

SCORE: _____ ÷ 10 X 100 = _____%

6. INTERPERSONAL THINKING

1. I get on well with my parents and siblings ◯yes ◯no

2. I need people around me a lot ◯yes ◯no

3. I form friendships easily ◯yes ◯no

4. I keep good friendships for many years ◯yes ◯no

5. I make use of different ways of communicating ◯yes ◯no

6. I find it easy to tune into the needs of others ◯yes ◯no

7. I find it easy to counsel and guide people ◯yes ◯no

8. People tend to come to me for counsel and advice ◯yes ◯no

9. I like to influence the opinions and/or actions of others ◯yes ◯no

10. I enjoy participating in collaborative efforts ◯yes ◯no

SCORE: _____ ÷ 10 X 100 = _____%

7. INTRAPERSONAL THINKING

1 I am very aware of all my emotions ◯yes ◯no

2 I am easily able to express how I feel in detail ◯yes ◯no

3 I can easily find different ways to express my emotions and thoughts ◯yes ◯no

4 I can sit quietly for hours on my own thinking and sorting things out in my own mind ◯yes ◯no

5 I believe I am very well-balanced ◯yes ◯no

6 I can work independently ◯yes ◯no

7   I am very organized   ○yes ○no

8.   I am motivated to set goals for myself and to achieve them   ○yes ○no

9.   I don't need people around me all the time   ○yes ○no

10. I prefer to be on my own to being in a group ○yes   ○no

SCORE: _____ ÷ 10 X 100 = _____ %

HOW TO HARNESS THE POWER OF YOUR "GIFT"

We all think differently. Each of us is a unique mix of each of the seven types of thought, and no two people on the planet have the same gift profile. We live in a world of diversely thinking human beings who are in relationship with each other; therefore, tolerance of different ways of thinking is necessary.

We all need to have each of the types of thought stimulated. The order of dominance of the 7 types of thinking just indicates how you think and build memory best and how to use your potential and gifts more effectively. This does not mean that you ignore the development of the one type of thought above the other; they are all supposed to work together. However, your top type of thinking literally gets the thinking and memory building process going – the top one is your "kick starter" kick starting the memory building process. Once this happens, then the thinking process starts to flow and the other types of thinking kick in to complete the cycle for full understanding.

If you are a teacher or parent or student, an awareness of all 7 types of thought becomes paramount, as this will guide you in seeing the unique gift in each person, including yourself.

For example, if kinesthetic is at the top of your thinking cycle, you will literally need to move around to kick start your thinking cycle and to get the other 6 types of thought flowing in order to understand and build memory. For some students in the traditional environment, this may mean they need to get up frequently to start this process. Your learning environment can be turned into a more kick start kinesthetic environment in the following ways:

»   Replace chairs with balls to sit on

»   Find out which of your learners or children needs to move and allow learners to move and stretch frequently

- » Play board games

- » Use your body to teach angles and geometry concepts

- » Teach integers on the playground by using hopping games

- » Put a treadmill or exercise bike in your office/learning area and walking while thinking

- » Play with a stress ball

- » Use an office chair on wheels that can spin around (take advantage of this!)

- » Go spinning at the gym or playing on a merry-go-round (this is excellent for the brain's concentration)

- » Use the Switch On Your Brain™ 5 Step Learning Process (See chapters 5 and 6)

Once you are working on this "kick start doorway" that quite literally opens up your gift, you also need to develop all of your cycle of thought to get your gift going.

Ways of "KICK STARTING" musical thinking are the following:

- » Play classical (not vocal) music CDs or tapes continuously in the background of your work environment

- » Have musical instruments (or make them – e.g. shaker's, percussion instruments) available and play them periodically

- » Do aerobic routines to music

- » Wear tap shoes and dance a rhythm with your feet in time to your fingers typing on the computer

- » Sing or hum while you work – even if it's under your breath so as not to disturb others

- » Read poetry

- » Pretend you are a disc jockey while you learn or work

- » Use the Switch On Your Brain™ 5 Step Learning Process (See chapters 5 and 6)

Ways of "KICK STARTING" visual/spatial thinking are:

»   Read cartoons (like Asterix and Obelix) and create your own

»   Examine ads and billboards

»   Use poster displays around your office or class to help you think and express ideas

»   Read poetry

»   Work with flow charts

»   Use mnemonic systems e.g. roman room, body parts, numbers and rhyme systems to remember and plan

»   Draw pictures or doodle when thinking

»   Use multiple visual aids e.g. posters, bulletin boards, technology, etc.

»   Close your eyes and see the situation or problem as a "movie" in your mind's eye

»   Practice differentiating colors

»   Take an art course

»   Make your food presentation attractive and colorful

»   Practice developing your visual memory by doing the Da Vinci exercise: stare at a complex object, memorize it, then close your eyes and try to recall it in as much detail as possible

»   Play imagination games

»   Play computer games

»   Use the Switch On Your Brain™ 5 Step Learning Process (See chapter 5 and 6)

Ways of "KICK STARTING" interpersonal thinking are:

»   Group work

»   Retell stories or tales

»   Use a thesaurus

»   Practice involving a group in your presentation or lesson – tune in to them

- » Practice making people feel at ease in challenging situations

- » Be friendly

- » Spend time with people

- » Listen without interrupting and planning your own response

- » Listen twice as much as you talk

- » Put yourself in another's position and try to think how they would think

- » Appreciate the uniqueness in others

- » Play around with questions

- » Learn from the greats

- » Expand your social environment

- » Take a presentation skills course

- » Deal with conflict by applying good listening and negotiating skills

- » Establish clear visions and missions for your team if you are leading, even in the classroom

- » Make sure all are aware of and agree with the direction you are heading

- » Deal with misgivings

- » Consider others' opinions and give them a "voice"

- » Give feedback

- » Acknowledge success and progress

- » Be aware of all the unique intelligence combinations in a group

- » Play "what if"games

- » Use the Switch On Your Brain™ 5 Step Learning Process (See chapters 5 and 6)

Ways of "KICK STARTING" your interpersonal thinking are:

- » Develop your intuition by listening to and becoming aware of it by being very still and silent

- » When your intuition is correct, analyze it

- » Develop your senses, which increases your awareness

- » Have quiet time and time alone

- » Write down dreams

- » Develop introspection, allow time for this

- » Associate new and unique ideas with old ideas

- » See things from different points of view

- » Respond as fully as you can to aesthetically appealing objects

- » Problem-solve and solution-find

- » Always see a situation as a challenge, no matter how bad, and find solutions to solve it

- » Self-talk

- » Take time to be with yourself

- » Be honest with yourself

- » Use the Switch On Your Brain™ 5 Step Learning Process (See chapters 5 and 6)

Ways of "KICK STARTING" your logical/mathematical thinking:

- » Practice estimating

- » Practice remembering statistics, those of your favorite sports team, for example

- » Use numbers to rank, organize and prioritize numbers

- » Play mental calculation games

- » Use your calculator as a training device and not a crutch!

- » Group together/chunk information you want to remember

- » Play games like backgammon and bridge, which are good mind sports

- » Be aware of how you use numbers automatically on a daily basis (e.g. how much time left till lunch, before work is over, etc.)

Conclusion

One of the best ways to develop your gift is to use the Switch On Your Brain™ 5 Step Learning Process presented to you in this book. This is a foolproof way of developing your gift in the best way possible for your own unique way of thinking.

Let's dive in!

Notes and Summary:

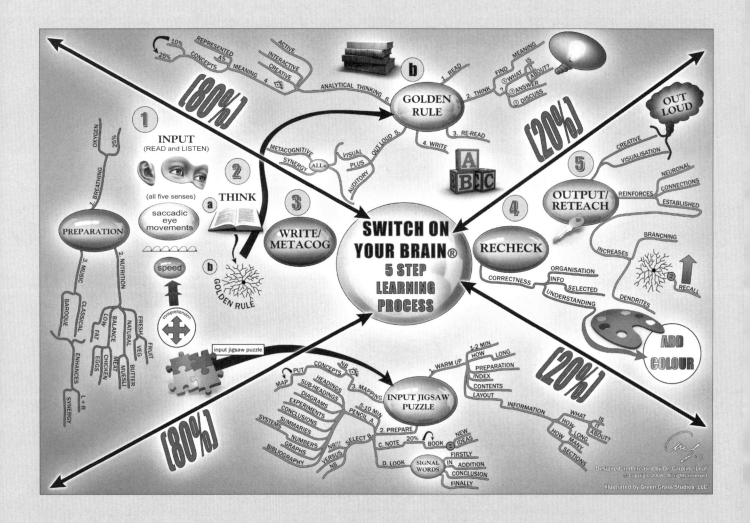

THE SWITCH ON YOUR BRAIN™ 5-STEP LEARNING PROCESS

"Thinking to understand" is the Golden Rule of the 5 Step Switch On Your Brain™ Learning Process. Without it, you won't learn effectively and you won't change your brain to release your intelligence.

Please note that I use the word "learning" throughout to mean building memory with understanding. Whoever you are and whatever it is you are trying to learn, you have to understand before you can possibly learn the information.

When you learn, you can be said to be in the "state of learning." In this state, you process information then store it for later use.

The Switch On Your Brain™ 5 Step Learning Process comprises 5 extremely important steps – none can be skipped. The system will not work properly unless all 5 steps are used correctly, because each is designed to take advantage of a particular brain process, with all collectively moving toward the goal of learning.

The five steps are:

1. *Input*: reading, listening, watching

2. *Think*: ask, answer, discuss

3. *Write*: creating the Metacognitive-Map®

4. *Recheck*: check for accuracy

5. *Output*: reteach

Each of the above steps plays a vital role in the building of memory, which is the learning process. Research shows that true mastery of new information and skills is based on strengthening the connections between the nerve cells in the brain, as well as on ensuring that the branches – the dendrites – that actually store the information are firmly attached (see chapter 2).

The easy-come, easy-go neuronal connections that come from rote learning and cramming for exams are quickly reversed, meaning they are forgotten. Maintaining improvement and creating memory banks of knowledge that can be used wisely requires the slow steady work that forms new strong connections.

The 5 Step Switch On Your Brain™ Learning Process does exactly that. Each step is meticulously designed to stimulate the correct chemical and electrical flow through the brain in the most efficient way possible to guarantee great memories.

As knowledge is developing and skills are building in the non conscious networks of the mind (the Metacognitive arena of the mind), it is not uncommon for the learners to feel that they are not making progress, but they simply must continue to "plug away" until the breakthrough comes.

Shortcut methods don't allow lasting memory and understanding to develop; it is the persistence of sustained thinking practice that solidifies the learning. This is because our thoughts can actually change the structure of the brain!

Research has shown the mental practice that comes from thinking deeply until an understanding is reached leads to actual physical changes in the brain. The mental practice of thinking is so powerful that researchers have taught people to play the piano through their imagination as effectively as someone learning the traditional way with an actual piano!

It is the systematic thinking-to-understand mental process captured within the Switch On Your Brain™ 5 Step Learning Process that will forever change the way you learn and stretch your potential to untold horizons.

This approach is solidly based on the latest scientific research on the neurological and neurophysiological functioning of the brain. It draws on the neuroplastic (ability to change) character of the brain and is designed to take best advantage of the symphony of electro-chemical reactions and actions occurring in the brain at a rate of 400 billion per second. One of the most exciting facts about the "plastic" brain is that the brain is never quite the same with every new piece of information we learn. This means that the brain can just keep getting better and better with the mental practice provided by the 5 Step Switch On Your Brain™ Learning Process.

THE 5 STEPS OF THE SWITCH ON YOUR BRAIN™ LEARNING PROCESS

STEP 1 Input.

The goal of input is straightforward – it is to understand what you are hearing, reading and experiencing, and to get the information into the brain properly. Information enters the brain close to an area called the entorrhinal cortex (see picture of the brain in chapter 8). The entorrhinal cortex is responsible for the preprocessing of the input signals (the information) and is an important memory center in the brain.

Here's how you can ensure that information is properly entered in the *input* process:

1. ***Always read with a guide*** – an instrument (pencil or pointer) to guide your eyes while you are reading. This could be your finger or a pencil or pointer – not a ruler or folded piece of paper or bookmark as these block the text. It will improve your concentration span and your comprehension by about 50 percent because it uses both sides of the brain at the same time. If you don't read with a guide, your concentration span will be shorter. You will think you are tired when you are not, because you are not using both sides of the brain at the same time, working in harmony.

2. ***Read out loud*** – you don't only need to see the words you are reading; you should also hear them. This auditory stimulation dramatically increases the possibility of understanding and decreases the chances of making mistakes in understanding the information being read.

3. ***Read a chunk of information at a time*** – a chunk is between one to three sentences long, bite sized amounts of information. We cannot build memory properly when we read through a whole section of work. Reading leads to a level of understanding but does not build long-term memory until we have understood the information. Easily digestible amounts of information, bite sized chunks, will lead to understanding because, like when you eat, you are digesting small amounts of information at a time.

4. ***Have the right attitude about what you read*** (review chapter 2 again where we explore how attitude works in the brain), because having the wrong attitude affects the chemicals and the electrochemical reactions, which will in turn, affect your understanding of what you are reading and slow you down. Be as interactive with the material as you can. See whatever it is you are about to read, whether book, notes, or article, as having been written by a person who is telling you something. Ask yourself what that person is trying to tell you? To understand the meaning of what you are reading, interact with words on the page as if you are interacting with whoever wrote them. To get into the habit of interacting with what you learn, ask yourself about the information, answer yourself by paraphrasing what you have read, and discuss it with yourself. This interaction allows the nerve cells to switch on the gene that makes good memories grow.

5. ***When listening, listen with a pen and paper and interactive thoughts.*** Here is how you listen attentively and intently to build good memories:

    »   Write down something – words, sentences, drawings – writing while listening is the important thing here. This forces deeper mental activity, which prevents your mind from wandering off.

» Get as interactive as you can – ask questions out loud or silently, repeat phrases the speaker is saying (silently to yourself, obviously), mentally discuss the topic to which you are listening.

» Control and discipline your thought life – there will be many intruding thoughts that are just there or that get stimulated by the information you are receiving. Acknowledge them, but don't indulge them until you have all the information you need from the person speaking.

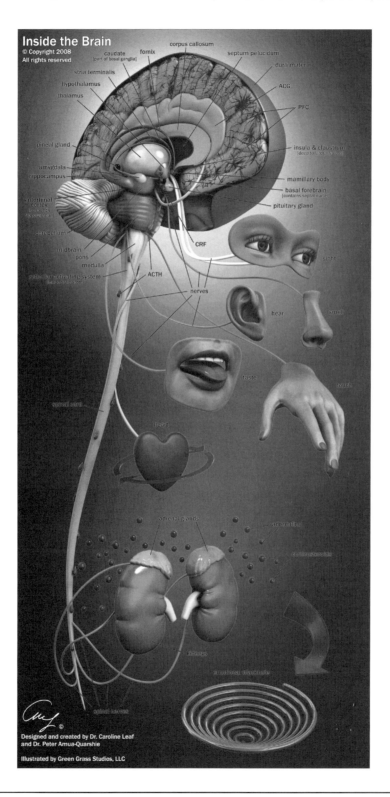

What's happening in the brain as you input information properly? As we explore this question, the drawing on page 56 will help you read through this.

As you input information into the brain by listening and reading and experiencing, the information passes through the areas in the region of the entorrhinal cortex, into the thalamus which is a relay station, sending all the incoming information up to the cortex (the outer part of the brain) where the memories are stored. Existing memories are activated, which will either help or block your ability to process the incoming information depending on whether they make you feel excited or anxious (see chapter 3). Your emotional state from the activation of these memories is fed back into a structure called the hypothalamus, which stimulates the release of chemicals to help with memory building. It's important to stay calm while in this process because anxiety will actually block memory building. From here the information passes into the amygdala (see chapter 2) where more preparation for memory building is done, and finally into the hippocampus – the structure where short-term memory is converted to long-term memory. This flow of electrical activity moves backward and forward in a looping way between all the above structures as the memory is starting to build. A lot is happening as you read and listen!

STEP 2: Thinking

The aim of the *thinking* step is to develop your phenomenal capacity and ability to exercise those neuronal connections and to get the nerve cells building and communicating fast and effectively. Before we even think of jumping into creating a Metacognitive-Map®, it is important to apply the Golden Rule of the 5 Step Switch On Your Brain™ Learning Process – to thoroughly understand the information you are trying to remember.

What is happening in the brain as you THINK?

The thinking step really challenges the brain to move into high gear, which is what the brain is designed for – deep intellectual thought. If your attitude is right, a level of expectancy builds and chemicals are released that will help the learning take place. Dopamine is released as the understanding is developing, and as mastery and understanding increases, endorphins are released. On a cellular level, protein synthesis is switched on when thinking hard to understand, meaning great memories are going to form. On a structural level, many different parts of the brain are involved in this thinking process: the corpus callosum is integrating information; the hippocampus is converting the information from short-term memory to long-term memory; the frontal lobe is making decisions and planning; the neurons are growing dendrites to store the information; and integration across the left and right sides of the brain is happening. Quite simply, thinking activates the gene that switches memory on and off.

So how do you think for optimal learning? Thinking is done by **asking, answering, and discussing** your way through each chunk (one to three sentences) of information. The end result of thinking is understanding; intentional thinking is essential to understanding.

Here's how you can optimize the *Thinking* step:

1. Read a chunk of information – between one to three sentences – out loud, with your guide (pencil or finger).

2. Ask yourself what you have read and answer yourself by rereading the chunk of information out loud, circling the concepts. Don't underline or highlight words. Those are passive actions, because they don't require you to think, analyze, or understand what you have underlined or highlighted. Circling is active.

3. Now, discuss the sentence with yourself, still looking at the sentence(s) you have just read. Discussion means you explain it to yourself over and over in your own words till you understand. If you can't work out what it means, ask someone or make a note to find out later.

4. As you are discussing, check how much you have circled. If it is more than 35 percent of a page, you have circled too much and probably don't understand fully. Go back and re-read and re-discuss until you can reduce what you have circled down to a maximum of 35 percent of the content. If you put more than 35 percent of content on to a Metacognitive-Map® (explained below), you probably think that if you put down lots of words, you will remember lots of them. Let me assure you, the opposite is more likely to happen. If you write down too many words, you will make your memory worse, not better. It is between 15 to 35 percent of the sentences that contain the most important concepts, the rest of the sentence words are filler words and don't need to be written down. Once you feel you have fully understood the concepts of the chunk you have just read, you are ready to make your Metacognitive-Map®. This involves writing concepts onto a sheet of paper in a way that is "brain-friendly." You will learn exactly how to do that below.

Now you have finished the THINK part, you are ready for the WRITING part.

STEP 3: Writing – METACOGNITIVE-MAPPING®

This step involves *writing* the information down in a brain-friendly way, called Metacognitive-Mapping®. This brain-friendly way of writing looks like the branching of a tree with leaves. Its pattern and shape are dictated by the pattern and shape of the actual neural network of the memory you are building as you analyze and understand information. It is really important to write as this reinforces the changes in the brain synapses at a microscopic level. As you think (step 2) you create changes in your brain; as you write down in the Metacognitive-Map® brain-friendly format, you reinforce and strengthen those connections. You literally grow your brain at will!

It is interesting to note that just by looking at a Metacognitive-Map®, you stimulate your brain to process information from detail to big picture and big picture to detail, which is vital to building strong memory. This only happens when both sides of the brain work together at the same time.

There is so much happening in your brain as you create a Metacognitive-Map®, that even reading about it can seem overwhelming. But it is truly fascinating!

As you use the tool of Metacognitive-Mapping®, the frontal lobe, parietal lobe, temporal lobe and occipital lobe all work together to integrate and apply the information. More neurotransmitters (serotonin, dopamine, norepinephrine and acetylcholine glutamate) are released from the brainstem traveling up through the limbic system (in the middle of the brain) into the cortex where the memory trees – the neurons – are found. The prefrontal cortex PFC – the outer front part of the frontal lobe – becomes very active keeping the information active in the neurons "in mind," monitoring and manipulating the contents of your short-term memory. The PFC works with other areas in the frontal lobe and the other lobes of the brain to make decisions, shift between the different bits of information, analyze, and so on. And, of course, a positive attitude ensures that genes are switched on for protein synthesis and good memories can form.

Because of the science behind them, Metacognitive-Maps® work for anyone and everyone. This is because they go much further than summarizing, note taking, or brainstorming. They allow you to extract, store, and later recall 100 percent of the information you need for tests, exams, presentations, and the application of skills.

When the two sides of your brain work together at the same time, you reach an important and deep environment of learning – the hemispheres of your brain do not work together when you read linear script. English is not the only language to embrace a linear script – straight lines in written form. Linear script can be from left to right, right to left, or even up and down in some languages.

However, reading from the center outwards is the big picture to detail, and that is your right hemisphere's way of processing. Your eyes will also read from the outer branches inward towards the center, moving from detail to big picture. That is your left hemisphere's ways of processing.

This act of creating a Metacognitive-Map® stimulates the corpus callosum to perform its natural function, that is, to get both sides of the brain working together integrating information across the hemispheres. That is why the Metacognitive-Map® is almost literally the "tool" that switches on the brain.

The Miracle of the Metacognitive-Map®

In earlier chapters you learned that the raw material of consciousness is made up of neurons (nerve cells with a cell body), an axon, and dendrites. When you listen, see, talk or learn, all this information goes into your brain as electrical activity. The more you stimulate your brain, the more you grow dendrites. When you learn using Metacognitive-Mapping®, you allow dendrites to grow in an organized linked way, across both the left and right sides of the brain. The denser, more organized dendritic growth there is in your brain, the more intelligent you become.

Your Metacognitive-Map® will look very different from other people's Metacognitive-Maps®, because everyone has a different learning style. Yours may be neat. Another person's may be messy. Yours may have lots of colors. Someone else's will have none. You may use more words. Someone else's will have fewer words.

Often, people think that you have to be visually oriented to create a Metacognitive-Map® and learn from it. In fact, that is the case with Mind Maps. But a Metacognitive-Map® is useful for everyone – whether you are visually oriented or not. That's because we all go through the same neurobiological process when thinking, learning, and creating memories.

Creating a Metacognitive-Map®

Did you know that that every time your brain sees a sentence, it isn't trying to remember every word? Rather, your brain instinctively tries to work out the essential 15 percent to 35 percent of concepts or information that is important. These concepts, or the essential information, are what you will write down on your Metacognitive-Map®. If you use more than that, you will have too many words to work with, and you will interfere with the memory of what is important. Between 15-35 percent is our ideal amount of information because less than 15 percent will cause gaps in your memory. Following the principles of creating a Metacognitive-Map®, in the correct sequence every single time, is an important part of successful learning.

Pay careful attention to the sequence of the following steps:

1. Start in the middle of a big blank piece of paper. Tape two letter sized pages (8x10) together as they can fold in half neatly and you can use both sides. You will be able to fit between 15 to 20 pages of notes on to two sides of letter-sized paper. Remember, you are putting everything you need on to the Metacognitive-Map®. That includes diagrams, maps, charts, tables, math examples, etc. so that you can do without your textbook or other pages of notes.

    In the center of your blank, white page, write the name of the chapter or section of work you are dealing with, for example, "climatology," "Russian Revolution" or "marketing plan for product X" in a circle or bubble (see examples in chapter 6).

2. Print all the words you put on to a Metacognitive-Map®. Don't write in cursive script. It is easier to remember something printed. Write the main categories in capital letters so they stand out. Write the detail in lower case.

3. Put the first sub-heading on a branch that radiates out of the central bubble.

4. Store all the rest of the information in concept form (don't write out full sentences) about that sub-heading, on lines branching from it – much like branches of a tree. The information you store should move from the general to more specific. This means that you "grow" branches outwards from the main category to accommodate the 15 percent to 35 percent of key concepts you have selected.

    Once you have selected and written down everything about that sub-heading, go to the next one and repeat the process until the whole section of work has been Metacognitive-Mapped®.

Take note: The shape of the branches you are growing on your Metacognitive-Map® will match the branches that you are growing in your brain on the "magic trees of the mind." Without you being consciously aware of it, your neural network will dictate the shape of the branches on your Metacognitive-Map®. That's why I say that a Metacognitive-Map® is your "brain on paper." As you draw the Metacognitive-Map®, your brain has already created the same pattern as a memory. If the words are all over the page, and not on logically connected lines, that's what will happen to the storage of information in your brain. It will be all over the place, and you won't be able to access the information when you need it for exams or presentations.

5. Start your Metacognitive-Map® in the top right hand corner of the circle and work around clockwise from left to right. You can go counterclockwise if it is easier. As we mostly work from left to right, the Metacognitive-Map® will follow the same format. You will need to rotate the page, so that you always work from left to right. In doing this, you will find half the Metacognitive-Map® upside down. This is actually a good thing because as you rotate the page, you promote synergy between the two sides of the brain. This turning of the page will also keep you awake and alert. It isn't wrong if you prefer your map to be read without turning it, but brain research shows that this crossing over is good for deep thinking. Finally, you will also find that it is more natural to rotate your page, as you instinctively like to work from left to right.

6. Apply the Golden Rule of thinking to understand how and when you select concepts. This law requires you to Ask, Answer, and Discuss. This is the conversation you need to have with yourself, as you learned above. You only want between 15 percent to 35 percent of information to go down on your Metacognitive-Map®. To make sure you get the essential information, you need to think about and understand what you are reading. You are not just trying to summarize information. You are filtering out what is superfluous and keeping only the relevant information. That's why you can eventually do without your notes and textbooks.

7. Each concept word must be on its own line. You literally build a sentence on branched lines, one word per line. You have to decide on logical, propositional relationships between the concepts you select. This relationship needs to be reflected structurally on the Metacognitive-Map®, which is why you need only one word or concept on a line. Words on linking lines lead to a spreading activation in which each concept triggers the next one in a logical and meaningfully associated way. This is what is happening inside your brain.

    More than one concept on a line interferes with the correct structuring of a Metacognitive-Map® and turns it into a type of flow diagram, or worse still, a linear summary.

    Another reason to put one word on a line is that each word has its own electrical representation in the brain. If you put two words on a line, it is the same as putting two electrical representations onto a dendrite (a branch of a neuron). The two collapse into one and half the meaning can be lost.

8. Use color simply to enhance organization at the recheck phase if you want to, but only after you have written down everything you think important. Your Metacognitive-Map® will be more visually appealing with rather than without color, but you do not have to put color on the Metacognitive-Map® if you don't like color. When you first make your Metacognitive-Map®, use one color, for example, a lead pencil, so you do not interrupt the flow of thought in your brain. It also makes it easier to erase if you have made mistakes, so you don't have to redo your Metacognitive-Map® altogether.

    Only add color in the Recheck phase, as a self-monitoring and memory-enhancing tool, if it helps you.

9. This step is entirely optional. Use pictures, symbols, shapes and images supportively to help with memory if, and only if, it comes naturally. You do not have to create an image for every word, but for groups of

concepts.

As in the use of color, it is better to put the pictures on to the Metacognitive-Map® in the recheck phase (step 3 below). When you concentrate on understanding and selecting 15 percent to 35 percent of the content, a picture may come to mind. If it does, you can put it on to the Metacognitive-Map®. Don't spend too long trying to create a superb image at the expense of concept selection. There is plenty of time to add pictures (the simpler the better), in the recheck and output stages. Pictures are helpful to activate the non-conscious levels of learning where intelligence or metacognition lie. However, the use of pictures and whether you use them at all, like everything else, will depend on your 7-gift combination (See chapter 4).

Remember you build a Metacognitive-Map®, so you read, ask/answer/discuss, and put the concepts onto the Metacognitive-Map® per chunk of information. Then you take the next chunk of information and read, ask/answer/discuss, and put onto the Metacognitive-Map®. Repeat this process until you have finished your Metacognitive-Map®.

STEP 4: Recheck

This is fourth step of the inputting stages of the 5 Step Switch On Your Brain™ Learning Process. It is important because it makes you check the Metacognitive-Map® you have created to see if it makes sense to you. You can't learn from something that doesn't make sense to you. This is a process of cross-evaluation of the content of your Metacognitive-Map®.

What's happening in the brain as you do this process? The slow steady work of the recheck step ensures that accuracy and consolidation have occurred in the neural networks by stabilizing the newly formed connections. The entire brain is challenged to work as an integrated whole, creating good communication among the neural circuits. This increases the flexibility of thought.

This recheck stage allows you to consolidate and reinforce memory of your work. It will soon become apparent if you have not fully understood what you are trying to remember. At this stage, you will have reread your work four times already and will be about to do it for the fifth time, probably without even being aware that you have gone over it so many times.

Your goals in the *recheck* process are:

>> Make sure you understand the Metacognitive-Map® you have made.

>> Make certain you are happy with the information you have selected, which will be in concept form. You can see whether you have too much or too little information, and whether the information makes sense.

> » Check whether you have organized the information in a logically associated way and check for cross-linking of information.

> » Check if you can make the concepts easier to remember by adding more pictures or symbols.

At this point in the Switch On Your Brain™ 5 Step Learning Process you will have stored information effectively enough, provided you have properly followed the rules of process to be able to access it later during a test or exam and to retain at least 60 percent to 70 percent of the information. To do even better, you need to move on to the final step of the 5 Step Switch On Your Brain™ Learning Process.

STEP 5: Output (reteach)

Output, the final step of the Switch On Your Brain™ 5 Step Learning Process, is only applied once you have been through all of the previous steps. It forms the final 20 percent of the whole 5 Step Switch On Your Brain™ Learning Process.

Remember that it will not help you just to read your Metacognitive-Map®. You need to teach it to yourself, to explain it out loud. Once again, that auditory and visual stimulation makes your brain work harder to form effective memory. Once you are happy with the reteach of your Metacognitive-Map®, then it is essential to get ahold of old tests, exams, papers, or assignments and test yourself.

The mental practice that happens in this output stage strengthens existing new branches just built into memory in the previous 4 steps as well as existing connections between nerve cells. This output step also creates new connections. This is because in the recheck, the new memories are consolidated and confirmed, and now in the output, the memories are integrated with other memories – new connections are made, leading to the ability to apply the information. The harder you think, the more connections are made. Useful knowledge is not just the storing of information, but the ability to link and integrate it with other information and to apply it (the 5 steps of the Switch On Your Brain™ Learning Process achieve this because each step is designed to build strong connected memories).

This step should be done two to three days before a test, exam, or presentation. Before that, you should go through the previous three steps daily or weekly, working through sections of information, Metacognitive-Mapping® them, and filing all your Metacognitive-Maps® in a system of your choice.

Elements that will make your output stage successful

Since this is the step where you reteach yourself, put your Metacognitive-Map® on a wall and

---

teach and explain it out loud to whoever is around and willing to listen to you. It can be a friend, a pet, or to yourself in the mirror. If you don't have a living being, you can even teach your pencil!

Here is the *output* process:

>> Reteach in the way that you would like to have been taught in class. This involves explaining what you have learned in detail and elaborating by way of extra examples. It involves imagining and seeing as though watching a movie of exactly what it is you are learning.

>> Paint a picture in your mind of the information on the Metacognitive-Map®. In other words make your Metacognitive-Map® come alive. Use your imagination – research has shown that imagination leads to great physical changes in the memory.

>> Continue reteaching until you can answer difficult questions without even looking at the Metacognitive-Map®.
You will normally have to go through the Metacognitive-Map® at least three times before you can confidently teach with full understanding better than your teacher or lecturer. It is at this point that you are ready to go into the test or examination, or to give the presentation, run the meeting or solve a problem, without looking at the Metacognitive-Map®.

If you find while re-teaching that something is not clear on your Metacognitive-Map®, then this is the time to look back at your notes or text and fix it up. After that, though, you need to put the book away, go back to your Metacognitive-Map® and continue.

Notes and Summary:

Chapter 6

EXAMPLES OF THE SWITCH ON YOUR BRAIN™ 5 STEP LEARNING PROCESS

In this chapter you will find examples of how to use Metacognitive-Mapping® (the key to the Switch On Your Brain™ 5 Step Learning Process) in selected subjects.

And keep in mind that you're going to be able to map out your very own Metacogs!

EXAMPLE 1: THE FROG

Summary of the Frog:

1. *Habitat*: Most frogs are land animals, but some types never leave the water. Frog eggs are laid in the water, and the tadpole is aquatic.

2. *Body Division*: Head and trunk.

   a) Head: Wide mouth; row of teeth in the upper jaw; long, sticky tongue attached to the front of the mouth; two protruding eyes with nictitating membrane; two nostrils for smelling and breathing; two round eardrums for hearing and balance.

   b) Trunk with two short forelegs and two large hind legs with webbed toes.

3. *Body shape*: Short, flattened from top to bottom; no neck and a hump on the back.

4. *Body covering*: Moist, naked skin with mucous glands and pigment cells.

5. *Locomotion*:

   a) Land: Jumps with hind legs.

   b) Water: Swims with hind legs and webbed toes.

6. **Breathing**: The adult frog breathes through his lungs, mouth and skin.

7. **Reproduction**: Oviparous; lays eggs in water where they are fertilized externally; tadpoles with suckers and external gills hatched by means of the heat of the sun; develop into tadpoles with a mouth, eyes and internal gills; hind legs appear later, then lungs develop; the front legs appear and the tail disappears; this change of shape is called metamorphosis.

Let's now look at the Metacognitive-Map® of the frog diagram. Study how I have made the Metacognative-map®® and apply the same principles to the other examples that follow, then try your own. Remember to watch the DVD that goes along with this workbook to help you.

TOP

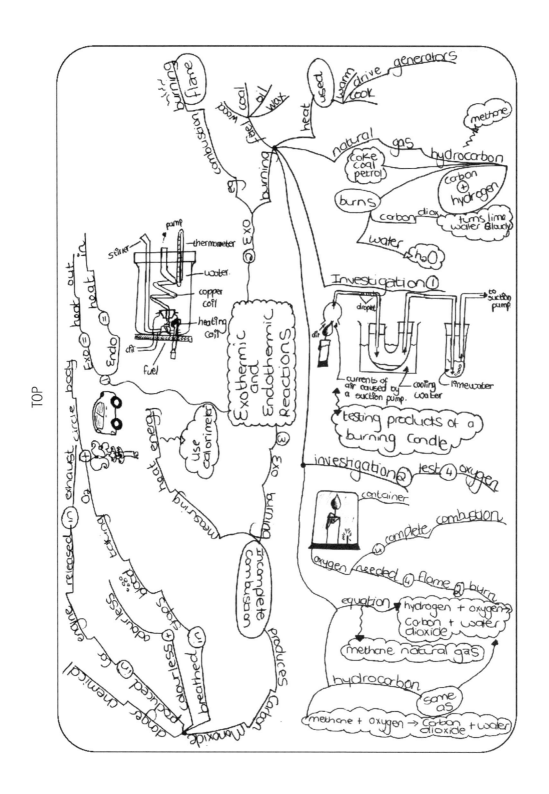

testing products of a burning candle

Investigation ①

Investigation ② test 4 oxygen

Exothermic and Endothermic Reactions

69

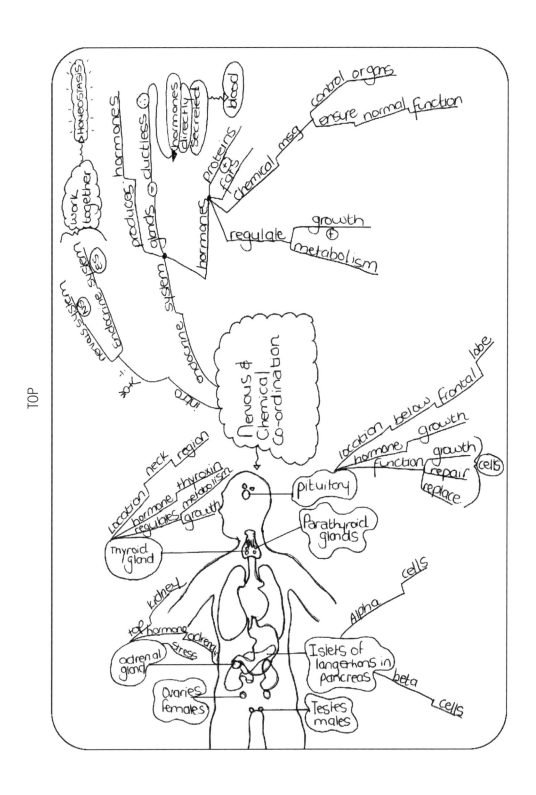

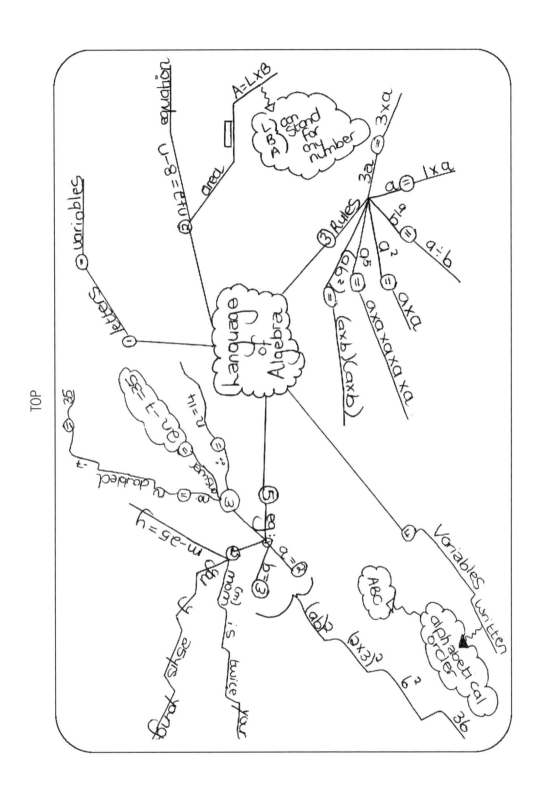

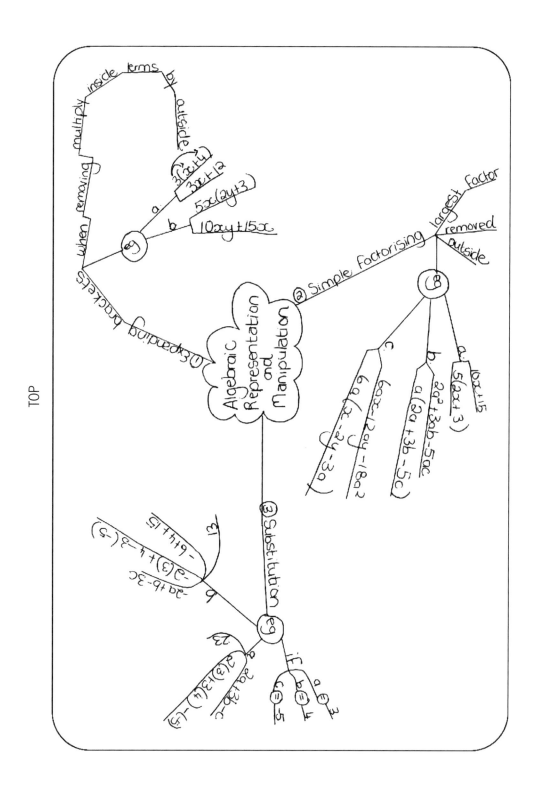

Algebraic Representation and Manipulation

① Expanding brackets
  multiply inside terms by outside
  when removing
  eg
    a 3(x+4)
       3x+12
    b 5x(2y+3)
       10xy+15x

② Simple Factorising
  largest factor removed outside
  eg
    a 10x+15
       5(2x+3)
    b 9a²+3ab-5ac
       a(9a+3b-5c)
    c 6axc-12ay-18a²
       6a(x-2y-3a)

③ Substitution
  eg
    if a=3
        b=4
        c=-5
    a -2a+b-3c
       -2(3)+4-3(-5)
       13
    b 2ab-3c
       2(3)(4)-3(-5)

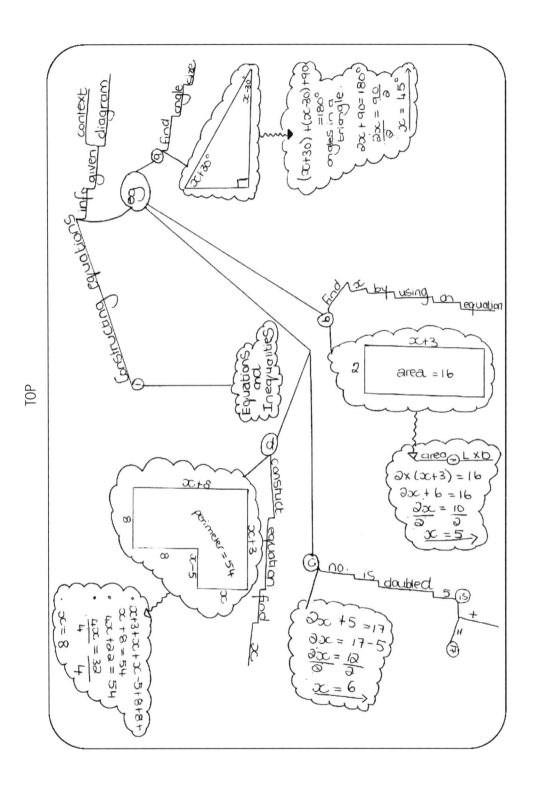

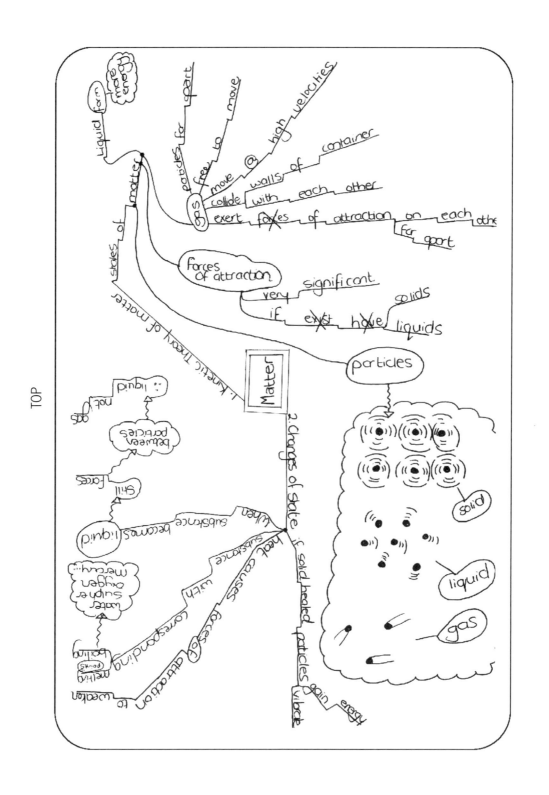

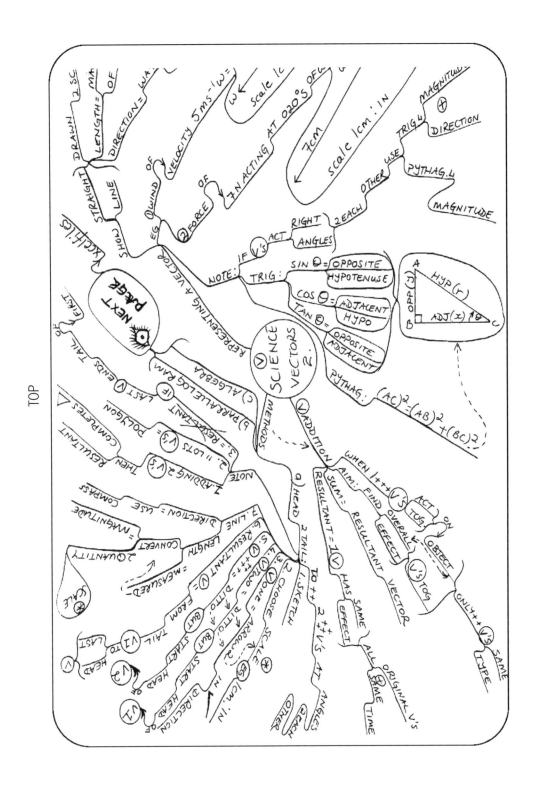

SCIENCE VECTORS 2.

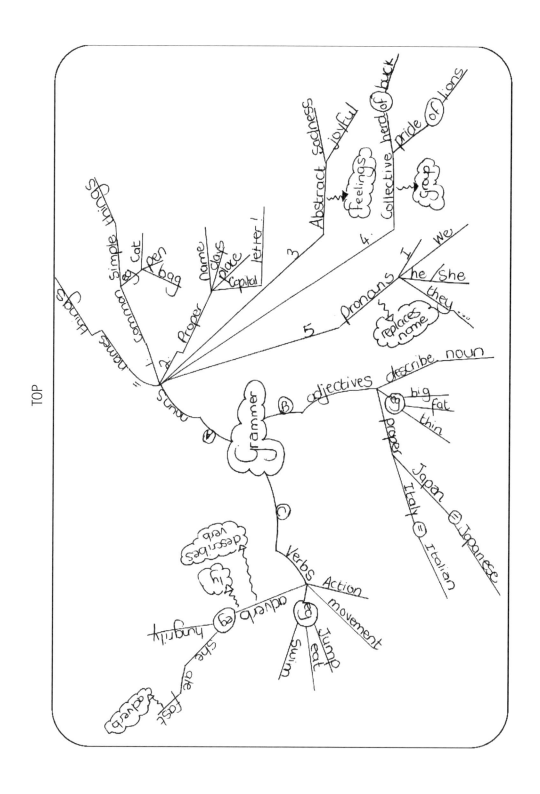

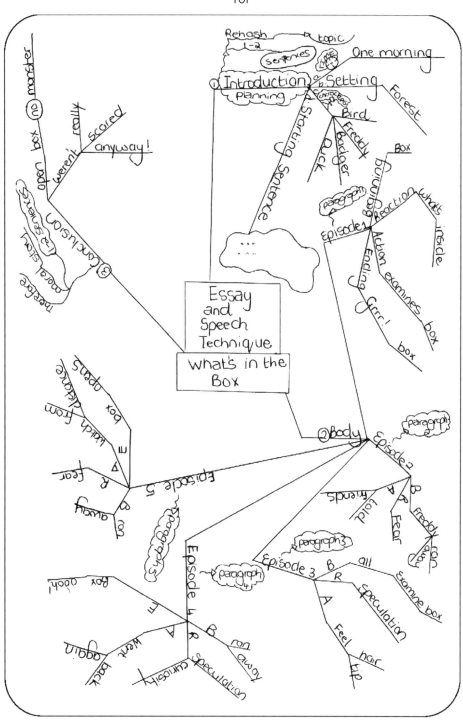

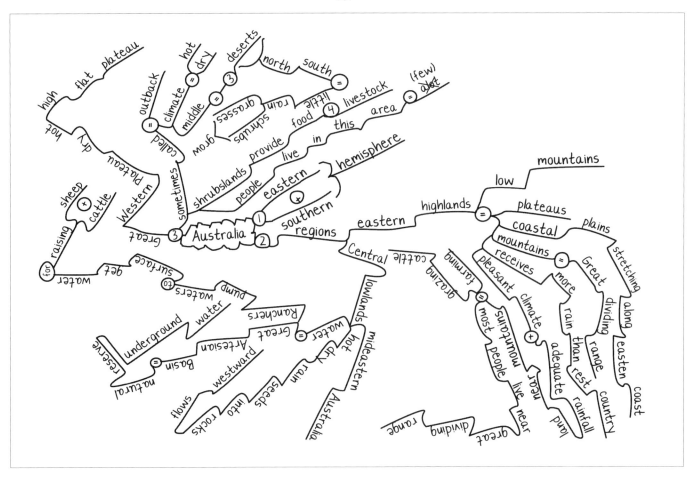

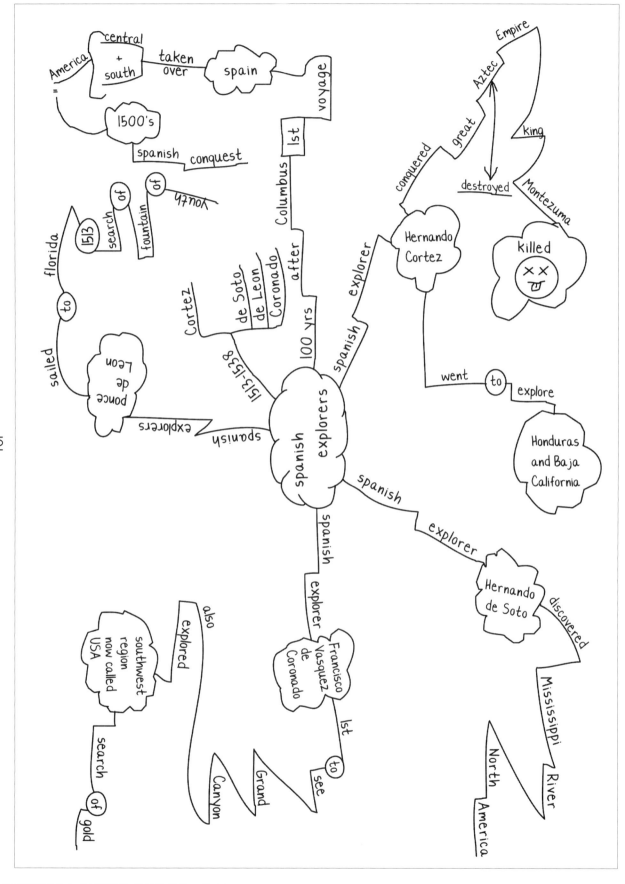

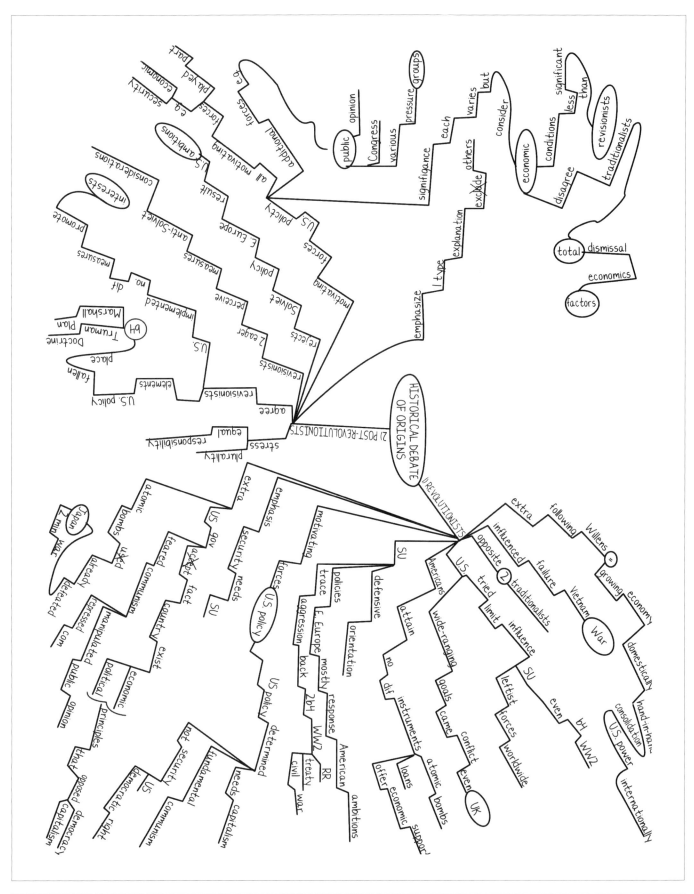

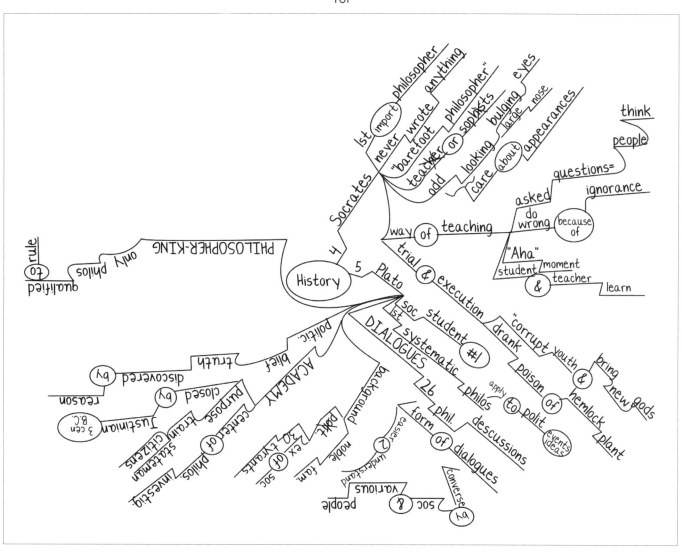

The mind map contains the following text elements:

Socrates branch:
- 1st (import) philosopher
- never wrote anything
- "barefoot philosopher"
- teacher of sophists
- add looking
- bulging eyes
- large nose
- care (about) appearances
- think people
- way (of) teaching
- asked questions = ignorance
- do wrong because of
- "Aha" moment
- student & teacher
- learn
- trial & execution
- soc student #1
- drank poison (of) hemlock plant
- "corrupt youth" & bring new gods
- apply to polit events ideas

History (center)

PHILOSOPHER-KING branch:
- only philos qualified to rule

Plato branch:
- 5
- 1st systematic philos
- 26 phil descussions
- form (of) dialogues
- background
- noble fam.
- ex (of) 30 tyrants
- easier to understand
- people various
- soc & converse (by)
- ACADEMY
- belief
- political
- truth discovered (by) reason
- closed (by) Justinian 3 cen B.C.
- purpose train statesman
- center of philos
- investig. citizens

81

Notes and Summary:

Chapter 7

ACING EXAMS WITH PROVEN TECHNIQUES

Exam words and Time Management

Solid exam skills can boost your chances of success in exams and also prove helpful outside of school. If your exam skills do not compliment your newly learned learning skill (*5 Step Learning Process*), you could end up undoing a lot of the good work you've done with the 5 steps.

When you improve your exam technique, you improve not only your chances of passing, but of acing your exam.

Once you've learned the process of the *Switch On Your Brain™ 5 Step Learning Process*, this exam technique will be easy to follow.

For example, when you are given an exam, whether multiple choice or essay questions, here are the most important steps to follow:

Prepare to Write:

Here's what you do when you first are handed an exam:

1. First allocate time per section. To do this, you need to:

2. Read through the entire exam. While you are reading, make marks alongside each exam question. With a double checkmark, check off questions you know you can answer well; use a single check for those you know fairly well; cross those of which you are uncertain. Start answering the double-checked questions first, then the single check, and last of all, the crosses.

    By answering what you know best first, you build up your confidence. By the time you finish those questions, you will often find that questions you initially thought difficult, no longer are. That's because you are in a better frame of mind.

3. Time Management of the Exam:

    •   Convert the time length of the exam into minutes
        (a three-hour exam, for example will be 180 minutes.)

    •   Look at the number of sections and amount of points per section.

    •   Work out how many facts you need to write per minute. For example, if the
        paper is three hours long (180 minutes) and there are three sections – A, B & C,
        the total point allocation is 300. You divide 300 (points) by 180 (minutes),
        which gives you 1.6. This means you must write approximately one and a half
        facts per minute.

    •   You now work out how long you have for each section. You do this by using the
        principle of proportion. Using the same example as above: If you see that section B
        has the highest point allocation – 150; A has 100; C has 50. If you allocate 100
        points per hour, this means you have 1.5 hours for section B, one hour for section
        A, and half an hour for section C. You must remember to take 5 minutes of each
        section for check each section for checking your work.

4. Always start with answering the longer questions, as these are more demanding and you
    need to be fresh and alert as you answer. Short questions are often more tricky. Students tend
    to spend too long on them and don't leave enough time for the long questions. Also, the tricky
    nature of short questions can stress you. If you are feeling stressed, you may battle with recall
    or information for the long questions.

5. Always spend at least 40 percent to 50 percent of your time for each long question planning
    your answer on a Metacognitive-Map®. After that, all you have to do is copy the information
    onto your exam paper in full sentences. Always hand in your Metacognitive-Map® with your
    exam paper. In other words, you do all your thinking, working out and planning on a Meta-
    cognitive-Map®. That way you will be 100 percent more effective in answering questions,
    as scientific evidence has proved.

6. When answering questions, look carefully at the way exam questions are worded. Look at the
    table on "exam question" words below:

1. Explain	how or why a thing works, the principle operating
2. Describe	provide word picture of appearance/nature of object or process
3. Define	provide exact meaning versus description
4. Discuss	give detailed points for and against proposition in question
5. Compare	explanation of differences and similarities between two or more elements and propositions
6. Enumerate	list the relevant points
7. Prove	provide facts and figures and evidence and supporting statements
8. Outline	briefly list the important ideas

Time Management

I'm often asked if there is a specific formula for study time.

It may seem surprising, but the amount of study time is important, and the length of breaks in-between study sessions is just as important to the Switch On Your Brain™ 5 Step Learning Process. Research on your body's biorhythms indicates that spending between 45 to 60 minutes is optimum in one go. After that, you should take a 5 to 15-minute break. After three sessions of learning you should take a longer break of around 2 hours.

If you try to learn for too long and don't take enough regular breaks, you literally "burn out" after 2 hours and waste the rest of the time you spend learning. You may think you are taking information in, but when you come back to the work, your recall will not be good – it can drop as low as 25-75 percent.

When you pace yourself according to this formula, you will be able to study for 6 to 9 hours in a day with excellent recall.

Time management for the five steps of the Switch On Your Brain™ 5 Step Learning Process works like this: during the term, you need to allocate 3-4 hours per week over one or two afternoons to do the first 3 steps:

1. Reading
2. Thinking
3. Metacognitive-Mapping®

Then the **RECHECK** and **RETEACH** steps happen two to three days before the test or exam. In other words, you make the Metacognitive-Maps® on a regular basis, but your exam prep is the recheck and reteach two to three days before the exam.

Notes and Summary:

Chapter 8

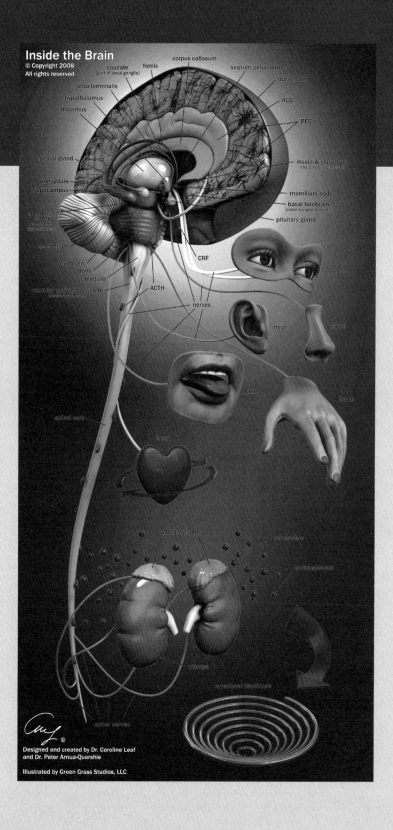

Inside the Brain
© Copyright 2008

corpus callosum
caudate
[part of basal ganglia]
fornix
septum pelucidum
dura mater
stria terminalis
ACG
hypothalamus
PFC
thalamus
pineal gland
insula & claustrum
[deep to this surface]
amygdala
mamillary body
hippocampus
basal forebrain
[contains septal nuclei]
entorhinal
cortex
pituitary gland
cerebellum
CRF
midbrain
pons
sight
medulla
reticular activating system
ACTH
nerves
hear
smell
spinal cord
taste
touch
heart
adrenal glands
adrenaline
corticosteroids
kidneys
emotional biochemic
spinal nerves

Designed and created by Dr. Caroline Leaf
and Dr. Peter Amua-Quarshie

Illustrated by Green Grass Studios, LLC

STRESS! CAN IT BE CONTROLLED?

Stress is rooted in fear, and when you are faced with things that make you feel as though you have lost control, you will experience fear and all of the strong emotions that accompany it. This can often create a mental block which causes us to either struggle through the learning process or only temporarily commit what we have already learned.

We have all experienced the situation where we go into an exam, panic and forget the answers, only to remember them once we have calmed down a few hours after the exam! This is because the stress chemicals actually shrink your memories temporarily, and you cannot use them until the stress chemicals have subsided allowing the memories to plump back up again. If we don't get the stress under control, over time the stress chemicals attack the memories and literally eat them.

Stress doesn't only affect our emotions or learning. It has an important impact on our bodies. How often have you had a sore tummy before going to school or just before an exam? This is because the digestive system is neurologically sensitive (responds to what you are thinking), causing the neurons in the stomach and colon to flare up in response to fear, anxiety and stress.

Stress is very real and has very real consequences – physical, emotional and intellectual. It can be controlled, but before I tell you how, you need to understand a little more about the science behind it.

At the root of all stress is fear. Fear comes from feeling out of control and can be caused by your schoolwork, exam preparation, inability to understand something, life circumstances, etc. What most people don't understand is that negative fearful thoughts – the root and fruit of stress – actually change brain chemistry. What's more, continuing such negative thoughts creates a stress response in our bodies, which rewires the circuitry of the brain over time.

If this happens in the young developing brain (birth to 19 years), it has the potential of forever changing the course of a person's life – unless that pattern is broken and the brain circuitry is intentionally renewed.

When it comes to actually dealing with stress, research has shown that young children up to the age of 18/19 years use their amygdala, a region that contains the emotional perceptions of memory and guides instinct and gut reaction; adults rely more on their frontal cortex, which guides deep analytical thinking and introspection. The young brain will tend to jump from sensation to reactive emotion, and this is where the damage comes in. The younger the brain, the more potential damage will occur. Damage will show up in many different forms and will manifest in even more ways and at different times. Symptoms can range from mild behavioral problems to complete mental blocking for self-preservation. These reactions can go on for years and will impact education as well as the emotional life of the child. Too often these days, we are seeing "educational casualties" coming through the system, underachieving and desperately unhappy – this is should not be happening. Approximately 70 percent of these children are stressed, depressed and some even suicidal.

We have already reviewed the importance of our attitude and how our thoughts affect our emotional, intellectual and physical state. The science behind stress cannot be more supportive of the need to break the cycle of negative attitudes or negative thoughts.

Stress – which is a very powerful emotion – sends emergency hormones flowing to the bloodstream, potentially causing brittle bones, infections and even cancer. If cortisol – the stress hormone – remains unregulated, it will affect your memories and intellectual thinking, and will make you sick. It can destroy appetite, cripple the immune system, and shut down processes that repair tissue, block sleep and even break down bone. We are damaging our brains and health unnecessarily with stress.

If negative mental templates become hardened into lasting strongholds that dictate behavior, you will be imprisoned or freed by the mental spaces you inhabit. So if you constantly think you cannot do something, eventually you won't be able to do it.

How can you make sure your brain circuitry is restored if you have negative thought patterns that cause stress? Since thoughts are mental activity mediated by electromagnetic forces and brain chemicals, called neuropeptides, when you change your thoughts, you can change the neuropeptides and electrical flow that dictate emotions and behavior. Change your thought patterns consistantly and you literally change the circuitry of your brain. This all relates once again to free will.

Let's review the three stages of stress and what they each mean to you as a student:

Stage One: Alarm Reaction

This is the "sweaty-palm, heart-beating-fast, adrenalin-pumping flight-and-fright" stage. At this point, all of your systems are still normal (believe it or not)! You have been created and are equipped to deal with protective levels of stress. These enable you to fight off a potential attacker or deal with a sick child, angry teacher, traffic jam, or any other difficult challenge life may throw at you. You actually go into a low level of stage one stress when you build memory – this is completely normal!

This acute short-term stress is necessary to keep you alert and focused in dangerous and life-threatening situations. It also takes a whole lot of effort for your body to do all these things to get you into the best possible physical and mental state to cope with the threat as well as the new learning and memory-building phase. This all helps you to feel alert and focused and is helpful when responding to challenges, such as making a speech or presentation, writing an important paper, taking an exam and so on.

The combined action of increased heart rate, the narrowing of the arteries, and the increased blood volume that occurs in stage one of stress is perfectly acceptable and manageable as long as it doesn't last for too long. If it does, however, instead of your body returning to normal, it shifts into the second stage of stress.

A GOOD POSITIVE MEMORY

"Spaghetti and Meatballs": microscopic slide of dendrite

Designed and created by Dr. Caroline Leaf and Dr. Peter Amua-Quarshie

Illustrated by Green Grass Studios, LLC

Stage Two: Here is where the problems begin

This is the stage where you start feeling physically unwell, with all sorts of vague symptoms. You may not be sick enough to stay in bed, but you no longer wake in the morning full of the joys of spring. You may also find it really hard to concentrate and remember at this stage. Your memory starts slipping, your thinking feels cloudy and your creativity levels are drooping.

This is the stage where the acute short-term stress you have experienced has turned into chronic long-term stress, which is not good for your brain or your body and especially not your schoolwork!

If you don't do something drastic at this crossroads stage, you will move into the last and potentially fatal stage of stress.

THE BLACK CLOUD: A NEGATIVE MEMORY CAUSING STRESS

A "toxic" memory

Designed and created by Dr. Caroline Leaf
and Dr. Peter Amua-Quarshie

Illustrated by Green Grass Studios, LLC

Stage Three: Exhaustion

Your body runs on hundreds of thousands of biochemical feedback loops. These are essential for homeostasis (balance in your body), the chemical and metabolic balance needed for all your bodily functions to work properly.

Toxic thoughts and emotions disrupt homeostasis and cause structural changes right down to the cellular level. Various stress chemicals are released into your bloodstream in growing amounts, causing your intellect and health to be severely compromised, resulting in emotional black holes (severe depression) and even death. The groundwork for this to happen begins when you enter stage one of stress. When the chemicals, as a result of prolonged stress, run wildly and build up, they begin to wreak all sorts of havoc on your health, both in body and mind.

That's why it is so important to keep a check on your stress levels and actively manage what chemicals are pumping through your system.

Once the stress is gone, the cortisol levels subside; the dendrites in your brain perk up and plump up again; your memory refreshes and your thinking clears.

Now you may understand why you went into that exam, and "blanked out," completely forgetting information you thought you knew so well, only to remember it when you came out of the exam. Many people find exam situations extremely stressful. Clearly, you cannot learn or perform optimally when fear hormones are pounding your body and mind. It's not overstating the case to say that in time, letting your stress hormones rule your body and mind is like being hit by tidal waves every time you try to build a sand castle on a beach.

At this juncture you will be really ill, maybe even hospitalized more often than you ever thought possible or necessary. You feel like giving up. Simple tasks feel like mountains to climb. You are spiraling slowly but surely into a physical and emotional black hole.

The fact is, all your organs have been in a state of heightened alert for just too long and have given up and become exhausted. Your adrenal cortex becomes enlarged. Your spleen and lymph nodes, thymus and immune system shrink. Your blood pressure increases. Your memory and mental functions dip drastically. You feel out of control, a failure, filled with self-doubt. Toxic waste has almost succeeded in all its dastardly deeds.

Fortunately, it's never too late to do something about what's going on inside your body and mind, and it is true that while there's life, there is always hope.

Tips on how to control stress:

1. You have to control your attitudes and thought life. Negative thinking and bad attitudes put your body into the stress reaction, which in turn affects your ability to think and learn. See chapter 3 on attitudes.

2. You need to know your work! This workbook provides a foolproof, scientifically proven and neurologically based system that will help you learn properly. The great thing about the Switch On Your Brain™ 5 Step

Learning Process is that not only will you learn how to learn and do better, you will also increase your intelligence!

3. Find a mentor that you can talk to and trust. You need to talk through all your emotions because they are living things that cannot be buried! Adolescence is one of the most stressful times in a person's entire life cycle, so let a reliable adult(s) help you through it. Your emotional reactions are not reliable as a teenager. Unless your emotions are dealt with, you will stress out, which will have a negative effect on your schoolwork.

4. Get enough sleep! At least 8 hours a night.

5. Eat properly (see Chapter 9).

6. Exercise at least 3 times per week.

7. Play and laugh a lot – this releases chemicals that calm you down and help build memory.

Notes and Summary:

Chapter 9

BRAIN FOOD

Besides conquering stress, there is another key that will help the Switch On Your Brain™ 5 Step Learning Process be most effective: eating well to feed not only your body, but your brain.

Scientists describe the brain as a "hungry organ," and it is the most complex organ in your body. Your body recognizes how important your brain is and treats it with the respect it deserves, giving your brain first bite of everything – at least 35 percent of the best of available nutritional resources from the food you eat. Your body can make some of the important nutrients your brain needs for proper functioning; others, it can only make from materials in the food you eat, which is why diet is so important.

To perform all of its functions well, it needs enough fuel to run on, and it can only get these substances from the food you eat and the liquids you drink.

Let's look at how what you put into your mouth affects your ability to think well. Everything you eat and drink affects your body, especially your brain. When your diet feeds your brain, your thinking will improve – the right foods help you to be more focused, alert and intelligent, and more stable in your emotions and behavior patterns.

Science is proving that the best diet is the way our ancestors ate – complete with protein, fat, and small amounts of complex carbohydrates from meats, fish, poultry, nuts, seeds, fruit and vegetables. Vitamins and minerals are also another very important component to ensure our brain is functioning properly.

Below is some helpful information about each of these essential components of a healthy diet:

Protein Power

One of the major problems with conventional dietary advice is an over-emphasis on carbohydrate intake and under-emphasis on protein. Protein forms the building blocks of the body's cells; builds, maintains and repairs all your bodily systems; and is responsible for growth and development throughout your life. You may also remember that protein is broken down by the body into amino acids and fats, all of which your body and brain need.

All your muscles, your immune system, your skin, hair and every cell in your body need protein for proper functioning. Your brain is no exception. Your brain needs sufficient quantities of high-quality protein to build solid memories. It also needs protein for neurotransmitter (chemical messengers) activity, because all your chemical messengers are made from amino acids – which are the raw material of protein.

Amino acids improve thinking by allowing neurotransmitters to transmit information speedily and effectively.

A deficiency in amino acids affects the ability of your neurotransmitters to help with thinking. It can make you depressed; apathetic; unable to relax; lacking in motivation, focus and concentration; and unable to build solid memory. Clearly that is not a desirable situation for your brain.

Good foods for your body and for your brain are the complete, complex protein foods with all the amino acids necessary for life. The best sources of these amino acids are those that nature provides in meat, fish, poultry, eggs, soybeans, and to a lesser extent, dairy products, preferably from free-range, organic sources wherever possible. Beware of those words "organic" and "free-range" though, as they have become overused and abused on the healthy eating scene.

Incomplete proteins found in nuts, brown rice, seeds and legumes, need to be combined with others to become complete. Brown rice and lentils, for example, combine to give you a complete protein.

Eggs have acquired an undeserved bad reputation for many years. They are a complete food, an excellent source of proteins and fats, and contain all the essentials for the growth of an organism – literally a super food. They contain amino acids in the closest thing to a perfect ratio.

It is a myth that eggs are high in bad cholesterol. That myth started 70 years ago when research sponsored by the Cereal Institute showed that feeding eggs to humans and animals would raise their cholesterol levels. However, this research was done using dried egg yolk powder. Dr. Taylor of Albany medical college pointed out that dried egg powder is an oxidized form that is toxic to the blood vessels; thus these early studies are invalid.

Eggs contain lecithin, a substance that is actually a good agent that lowers "bad cholesterol." Eggs will reduce rather than increase your bad cholesterol!

They have other benefits. The lecithin they contain has choline in it, in the form of phosphatidyl-choline. Choline is a B vitamin needed for transmission of electrical charges across synapses. It is the substance from which acetylcholine, the memory neurotransmitter, is directly made, so eggs help your memory and intelligence.

It is true that the nutritional content of the egg depends on how well the chicken has been fed, but that's all relative. Along with organ meats, eggs contain high-quality protein and are the richest source of phospholipids (fats) in average diets.

We shouldn't be worrying about proteins, rather we should be making strides to reduce carbohydrate intake and drastically limit the bad, damaged fats that are abundant in processed and refined convenience foods.

Fat Chance

Your body needs fats in the diet for all its processes, and so does your brain. Your brain is actually made up mostly of fat – 70 percent when you take out all the water in it. Fats protect you from disease. They balance your mood, make you more focused and able to concentrate, and maximize your intelligence.

Fats come in different forms:

- » Saturated, unsaturated

- » Mono- and polyunsaturated

- » Cholesterol

The saturated fats in fatty protein foods are good for you. These foods quickly and easily stabilize blood sugar levels, provide the amino acids necessary as the building blocks of the body, contain fats the body is designed to cope with, satisfy the body, and settle hunger centers.

For overall health, your body can make most of the fats it needs except Omega 3 and 6 fats, known as essential fatty acids (EFAs). These fats lower blood pressure, boost immunity, help insulin to work, and regulate the neurotransmitters in the brain helping to improve learning and attention. These EFAs are needed in the unheated form. When heated they attack your nerve cells, having a negative effect on memory. Good sources of Omega 3 and 6 are flax seeds and oil and sunflower seed and oil – unheated of course.

Good sources of phospholipids in the diet are eggs (because of the lecithin they contain) and organ meats.

Unlike vitamins and minerals, EFAs and phospholipids have no recommended daily allowance for fats. All indications are that you can't easily overdose on them. The best sources of EFAs and phospholipds are cold-water oily fish, such as sardines, salmon, mackerel, pilchards, herring, trout, and tuna (fresh, not canned because the oils have been extracted), and cold-pressed vegetable oils such as flaxseed, hemp, safflower and sunflower oils.

Carbohydrates

Carbohydrates are breads, pastas, potatoes, fruits and vegetables. You only need small amounts of complex carbohydrates. These are foods in their natural, unrefined, unprocessed state, and they release their sugar content slowly into the body. This is ideal to maintain your health and weight and to allow your body to make glucose available for delivery in a slow and steady stream to the brain through the bloodstream.

Whole grains, vegetables, beans and lentils are complex carbohydrates and a good source of fuel for the body. Protein foods such as meat and chicken also contain complex carbohydrates, in sufficient quantities to meet the body's needs. They contain both saturated and unsaturated fats, which your body can use along with the protein as fuel sources and to make other substances available for proper functioning.

There is agreement among nutrition scientists that simple, refined carbohydrates such as white bread, pasta, and processed cereals are not good fuel sources because they release their sugar too quickly. Their chemical composition once metabolized is not much different from that of pure sugar and is often referred to as "white poison" because when used in excess, it negatively affects the body. These types of foods continually force your body to compensate by making the pancreas produce excessive amounts of insulin, the hormone needed to metabolize sugar and carry the necessary amounts of glucose into the cell.

It helps to get to know the Glycaemic Index (GI) – a list of foods rated according to how fast or slow they release their glucose content into the bloodstream. It's an invaluable aid to devising brain-boosting menus.

Vitamins and Minerals

Vitamins and minerals are the brain's master tuners and must not be forgotten. They play a very important role in metabolism, turning:

- » Glucose into energy

- » Amino acids into neurotransmitters

- » Simple essential fats into more complex fats like GLA and prostaglandins

- » Choline and serine into phospholipids

A high intake of refined, processed foods and sweetened, fizzy drinks forces the body to compensate to cope with all the foreign chemicals coming in from the "junk" food. This will be at the expense of concentration and intellectual functioning.

Vitamins and minerals help build and rebuild the brain and nervous system and keep everything running smoothly. It has been proved that intelligence will increase with an optimal intake.

You will think faster and concentrate longer with an optimal intake of vitamins and minerals. A multivitamin and mineral supplement should give you at least 25mg of all the B vitamins, 10mcg of B12, 100mcg of folic acid, 200mg of magnesium, 3mg of manganese and 10mg of zinc. Something like Barleygreen or a good food-state vitamin will supply this and more, positively influencing the endocrine system and hormone production.

Brain recipes for good thinking

Eating to increase your intelligence is really quite logical. Eat a wide variety of foods, from the three food groups of proteins, fats and carbohydrates and avoid refined, processed, pre-packaged foods and fizzy drinks as much as possible. You don't have to cut them out altogether, but to be a clear thinker, you should only have them once a week at most.

If you are going to live on a diet of chocolates, sweets, cake and carbonated drinks, you are not going to have a brain functioning at optimal chemical levels.

Now that we have a better understanding of each of the important groups in a diet that feeds our brains, here are some specific "brain food" tips:

- » Never skip breakfast: always eat protein for breakfast; it triggers the release of excitatory neurotransmitters, such as norepinephrine and dopamine, needed for clear, fast, concise thinking and memory. Good choices are eggs, fish, turkey, chicken, yogurt. Whole-wheat toast, spelt or essene bread, fruit, rolled oats are also healthy choices. Lack of sleep and too much stress deplete dopamine levels, so it is important to replenish them with a power-protein breakfast after a hard night's learning.

- » The night before a test or an exam: if you are worried that you won't sleep well before an exam, you can eat mostly unrefined carbohydrate-rich food, such as spelt, rice or whole-wheat pasta.

» A nibblers diet is best for the brain: eat small, frequent meals. Small meals enable learners to maintain better insulin levels lower cortisol (the stress hormone) levels, and better glucose tolerance, which in turn, leads to improved thinking.

» Eat iron-rich foods: when your iron levels are low, your physical energy levels will be low, as will the activity levels of your brain. Iron-rich foods are dark green vegetables, meat, beans, fish, poultry, grains and rice. Vitamin C sources (orange juice, broccoli, bell peppers) enhance iron absorption. Phytates (cereals, brans) and tannin are shown to inhibit the absorption of iron into the bloodstream. If you have a breakfast of orange juice, fruit and eggs, you will absorb five times as much iron as with cereal, bran and eggs, and coffee or tea.

» Remember the Bs: eat foods high in B vitamins, among them thiamin (B1), riboflavin (B2), folic acid, and pyridoxine (B6). Research shows they are critical for brain and nervous system health. Meat is an excellent source of B vitamins and only needs to be eaten in small quantities. Vegetarian sources include wheat germ and nuts. Symptoms of B vitamin deficiency include short or limited attention span and memory loss.

» Drink enough water: water is as critical for brain performance as it is for your overall bodily health. Brain specialists advocate drinking between 6 to 8 glasses of water per day, depending on your body size, activity levels, and the weather. The average learner is walking around chronically dehydrated, which negatively impacts learning performance. Sipping on water all day long can improve intellectual performance and behavior fairly dramatically in some cases. The water must be from a clean source, as drinking water and many mineral waters have heavy metals in them. Use reverse osmosis filters for your water.

» Eat fresh fruits that are in season in controlled quantities: the fructose they contain is a sugar, but a slow releasing one. Bananas release their sugar content quickly, but they do contain lots of sodium and potassium shown in research to be important in memory formation at the synapses.

» Supplement use: it's important not to incorporate unneeded vitamin and mineral supplements, especially without consulting with your doctor first. In fact, when your diet is properly aligned with the nutrition that you need, you shouldn't need outside supplements. A healthy diet includes lots of fresh foods from organic, free-range sources and will provide the nutrients you need, unless you have a medically identified deficiency. Many of the foods you eat are rich in anti-oxidants, especially dark orange vegetables, such as carrots and sweet potatoes, or dark green leafy vegetables like kale and spinach. Supplements like Barleygreen and wheatgrass in powder form, on the other hand, are closer to food than supplements because they are not made up from, single molecules. Algaes are also whole foods.

» Coffee is fine with moderate intake: 3-4 cups of fresh brewed or filtered and preferably not instant (artificial with too many chemicals). Filter coffees and cappuccino or espresso containing complex carbohydrates are best.

» Avoid alcohol: it is shown to slow down brain function.

» Don't use aluminum cooking utensils and don't drink fruit or other juices packaged in aluminum-lined cartons. Don't use tin foil. These heavy metals affect brain function.

» Don't use "spray and cook" type substances as these are poisonous, more so than pesticides, and stay in your body permanently.

» Make sure you get enough protein and unheated fat in your diet.

» Use full cream milk and pure butter – avoid margarines as they are heated fats and are bad for your brain.

» Cheese: mozzarella is one of the best because it is boiled.

More products by Dr. Caroline Leaf available at: www.DrLeaf.net

Notes and Summary: